"Adele's advice has been a **constant sou**
journey of blending our 2 families. I
then I had guilt on top of those feelings m
know that what I was feeling was "normal" or common . now i know y
see light at the end of the tunnel. Thank you."

—Cathleen Y. Waukesha, Wisconsin

"Adele, **I don't think I would have made it this far in my relationship if it wasn't for**
the info you gave me. I don't know if your timing was on purpose but I can tell you I was
ready to leave the relationship and praying to God to give me a sign for what to do. That's
when I received your emails on what love is and how to stick it out if you love that person
and that if you bail out your next relationship will have the same problems. THANK YOU
for your help. I know this is a work in progress, but I'm definitely going to give it my all and
God willing we are going to be a family!"

—Bob Kremer, New York

"Thank you so much! We are loving it. We can't either one seem to put it down. **We are**
laughing and crying, and wondering if you have been following us around for the
past year and a half...recording all of our mistakes. Ha ha!! We have made them
all! My husband was wondering if you have been living with us! Thank you! Thank you!
Thank you!"

—Patty Johnson

"The information is very **useful to help in the transition with my girlfriend and**
her son. It's been a little rocky to say the least, **and the advice given helped us out**
immensely. I can sit down and not feel neglected, and actually talk about things with my
girlfriend regarding her son's words or actions. I can convey to her how I feel and she takes
that to heart and really tries to make it work. Thank you for guidance!!"

—Benjamin Garcia, Jr, Carson, California

"I really appreciate receiving Adele's advice. **It has helped me to continue looking at my**
relations with my husband and his children. I look for areas where I can improve my
actions and reactions. I can not control theirs but I appreciate the advice that has helped me
to look into myself. **It has helped to know that I am not the only one out there dealing**
with step family problems. Thank you for all of your guidance and advice."

—Dea Lott, Idaho Falls, Idaho

"*Every time I receive your information Adele, it is like opening a gift from a dear friend. I am a childless step mother in a blended family and have often felt lonely and isolated in my home because of being the outsider to this family.* **Your advice and the contributions from the blended family members speak to me in a way no one else would understand.** *I feel as though I belong to an exclusive club no one else would want to belong to and yet I value it more than any other organization of which I am a member. Thank you.*"

—Julia Phelan, Toronto, Canada

"**Since I discovered Adele's information online there has been a lot of peace and understanding in my life**. *Her advice is amazing and I would recommend it for newly blended families and blended families that have been together for years already. It helps you decipher certain feelings within and what to not take personal when dealing with ex's or step-children, and people from the past. Through Adele's knowledge I learned to just be accountable for myself and to be a better more understanding role model for all six kids. I feel really blessed to know Adele and to have used her information, which I will continue to do so. I wish there were more caring people like her that understand what we go through as Second Wives, Step-parents, and People in general. Thank you for all your help in changing my way of thinking and for making me feel I'm not alone in the World of Blended Families. God Bless.*"

—Barbara Rodriguez, Youngtown , Arizona

"*Adele is a* **tremendous resource of help for blended families**. *The insights found in this manual are* **a must read** *for every blended family. Adele deals with the difficult issues stepfamilies face and* **provides significant solutions**. *Her worksheet format equips people to apply what she teaches.* **Adele shares as a professional and as someone who has worked through the struggles of living in a blended family.** *I am thankful for her commitment and encouragement of people all around the world who are working to help blended families.*"

—Dr Shane Stutzman, President of Doing Whatever It Takes Ministries/Pastor Eastside Baptist Church, Orlando Florida   www.doingwhateverittakes.org

To receive free weekly tips plus ongoing support and advice on the subject of blended families including:

- ◆ Ex-partners
- ◆ Healing after divorce
- ◆ Helping children thrive
- ◆ Personality profiling

Go to:

www.StepFamilyHelp.info

FREE GIFT!
ebook valued at $19.97

Blending
The Hidden Truths

Discover what men and women say about:

- ◆ The one thing they want to change in their blended family
- ◆ What they feel guilty about and how it influences their parenting
- ◆ How their feelings affect their commitment to their relationship

Plus:

I'll tell you:

- ◆ The two types of guilt and how to overcome them
- ◆ Advice to use if your spouse doesn't want to bond with your child
- ◆ Why some families succeed and others don't
- ◆ What to do if you don't "feel" love for those around you
- ◆ The three types of love and what love *really* means

To access your bonus gift, go to:
www.StepFamilyHelp.info/1bonus

A catalogue record for this book is available from
the National Library of New Zealand.

Published by:
Omega Trust
PO Box 30-629
Lower Hutt
New Zealand

First edition June 2008
Copyright © 2008 Adele Cornish

Email: adele@stepfamilyhelp.info
Website: www.stepfamilyhelp.info

All names have been changed to protect individual identities

Cover design by Fran Linden

Layout and typesetting by JustYourType.biz

Printed and bound by Publishing Press, Auckland, New Zealand

Blended Family *Success*

Practical Solutions to Step Family Challenges

ADELE CORNISH BSW

Acknowledgements

This book would not have been possible without the hundreds of blended families worldwide who have shared their personal journey with me. A huge "Thank-you" to each of you for your openness and honesty. I would also like to make special mention of those who graciously gave me their words of encouragement at the front of this book.

I am most grateful to my children and stepchildren for their support and patience while I've been working on this project and particularly my husband Mike who has always believed in me, encouraged me and given me the opportunity to 'dream big' and pursue my vision.

There are some more very special people I wish to thank. Colin Salisbury has been instrumental in getting this book written though his advice, brilliant skills and practical assistance. Leanne Hourigan and Martine Bergman; this book would have taken an extra 10 years without their practical support and generosity in minding my children! Their spontaneous help freed me up to work and write often in such a timely manner.

I'm also very grateful to my friends who have helped, encouraged and supported me to press on over the past few years to bring this book into fruition. Erin Cassidy who initially gave me a note book which has been invaluable for jotting down my thoughts and clarifying my direction. Kate Dominikovich, an amazing lady who has contributed her wisdom and encouragement. Others just as important who have encouraged and prayed for me along this journey are Angela Holmes, Sarah Malone, Liz and Doug Pa'u, Tara Connell, Jo Salisbury and Dianne Bryan.

Last but not least, thank you to my in-laws Margaret and Cecil Marshall, my father and stepmother, Ron and Marion Candy and my terrific aunt, Shona Bowater who have all encouraged and supported me in fulfilling this vision.

Contents

Introduction...XI

PART 1   HOW TO HAVE A FANTASTIC RELATIONSHIP 1
Success Strategy

    1   Setting Priorities: Putting your spouse first 3

    2   How to Have Intimate Communication...7

    3   Feeling and Showing Love..10

    4   Two Crucial Keys to a Fantastic Relationship.....................................14

    5   Overcome the Barriers to Intimacy 17

            -   Manipulation

            -   Dishonesty and Criticism

            -   Jealousy

PART 2   RESOLVING CONFLICT...25
Success Strategy

    1   How Experiences of Conflict Affect Behaviour...................................27

    2   Styles of Resolving Conflict 30

    3   How to Listen Effectively 33

    4   How to Avoid Criticism 35

    5   The Power of Emotions!...41

    6   How to Overcome Past Hurts 45

    7   Steps to Resolve Conflict 51

    8   Who Should Have the Ultimate Say? 53

    9   Help with Financial Conflict..56

PART 3   EFFECTIVE BOUNDARIES.. **61**
Success Strategy

1   Parenting Styles: Identify your own 63

      - Opposite parenting styles? What to do

2   Setting Boundaries 67

      - Who's in control in your home?

      - Guilt: The biggest barrier to discipline!

3   How to Discipline: The Five Steps...74

4   Teaching Consequences...77

      - More strategies for success

      - Evaluate your system: How effective are you?

5   Presenting a United Front..83

6   Parental Responsibilities 87

      - Strategies to help each other succeed

      - Different homes different rules: How to cope

PART 4   SECRETS TO SUCCESSFUL PARENTING **93**
Success Strategy

1   Help for Biological Parents 95

      - How to overcome guilt

      - Torn between your spouse and children?

      - Overcoming divided loyalties

      - Strategies to use when feeling torn

2   Positive Step Parenting 100

             - Tips for those who haven't parented before

             - Understanding the difficult stepchild

             - A crucial key to successful stepparenting

             - Conquering resentment!

             - The role of a stepparent

3   Meeting Children's Needs 112

             - Using time wisely

             - How to treat children equally

             - Another secret to success

4   How to Bond with Stepchildren 118

             - Loyalty: A child's and parent's perspective

             - Steps for stepparents

             - How biological parents can help

Closing Comment..**126**

Bibliography **128**

About the Author..**129**

Dedicated to the One who gave me this vision.

Introduction

According to Statistics New Zealand, just over one-third of all marriages in 2005 (7,300) were remarriages of one or both partners. About 90 percent of those remarrying had been divorced. It's estimated that around a quarter of families in New Zealand are remarriages with children. Statistics from one Christchurch study found that 53% of remarriages had dissolved within five years although counsellors estimate this figure could be closer to 75% across New Zealand (1).

Welcome to the world of blended families! First I'll let you in on a secret that few people are aware of - it takes on average seven years for a blended family to build relationships and function as a genuinely united team (2). That's right, seven years! It can happen faster if parents are proactive in bringing everyone together but may be longer if they aren't. If the statistics above are anything to go by, most blended families don't hang around this long. To succeed, you need to wait patiently for family members to become familiar with expectations and comfortable in their role. Blended families don't function in the same way as a nuclear family (where both biological parents are present). Divorce reorganises a family spreading it over two households. However, the primary emotional blood ties remain the same despite the change in structure.

Every blended family faces challenges; most don't manage to work effectively through them. Risks for children in stepfamilies are similar to children in single parent households who experience poorer outcomes compared to those in nuclear families. Until now there has been a lack of resources available to target the specific needs of stepfamilies. Here's your chance to finally get some help. Blended families are plain hard work at times but using the skills, strategies and principles outlined here you can turn your family into a successful and supportive team! Yes, there is hope for your family. So, despite what you're feeling or where you're at right now, be prepared to put in some effort and you'll start enjoying your family life!

(1) John and Agnes Sturt, *Mentoring for Marriage*: A resource manual for Pastors, Counsellors and Couples (Auckland: DayStar, 2003) p.160

(2) Patricia Papernow, *Becoming a Stepfamily*: Patterns of Development in Remarried Families (New York: Gardner Press, 1993)

To receive ongoing support and advice on the subject of
blended families, go to:
www.StepFamilyHelp.info

Part One

How to Have a Fantastic Relationship

Your marriage relationship forms the foundation for your blended family's success.

Imagine: You've spent the past 2 hours preparing the dinner, cleaning the room, setting the table and you're all about to enjoy a blissful blended family meal together. But wait! Sally starts whining because she wants to sit next to her daddy and you're in the way, Peter (your own son) tells Sally not to be such a baby, Tory's complaining because she hates your cooking and to top it off your partner starts yelling at everyone. Instead of the bonding family dinner you planned, you're suddenly smacked with the reality of stepfamily life!

Every parent in a blended family will tell you children put expectations and loyalties to the test. If you've got a strong relationship, you'll get through these challenges and not end up another divorce statistic. Your blended family's success largely depends on the strength of your marriage. The challenges you face concerning children will be easier to work though if you've taken the time to establish a firm foundation.

You can enjoy a healthy, fulfilling family life if you are prepared to work at it; just don't expect it to happen automatically! Now that you have found the right partner, it's really important to shift the focus to *being* the right partner. You may find it easier to identify the faults in your spouse without stopping to reflect on your own. Here's your chance to look individually and together at what each of you can do to create a healthy and successful marriage relationship. Part 1 and 2 of this book will help you build and strengthen your foundation then we'll focus on the challenges of raising children in a blended family.

Strategy 1: Setting Priorities

In a relationship without children, a couple has the luxury of uninterrupted free time together. Their focus is on meeting each other's needs. It's the little things they take for granted such as no bedroom intruders. Once children arrive, they don't have the same freedom to in indulge in uninterrupted time. The focus naturally goes on the kids, particularly so for 'mum' who is often responsible for meeting their day-to-day needs. Many couples believe children will bring them closer together but sometimes it can cause the opposite. Although almost every parent enjoys and loves their children, the change in lifestyle, sometimes less income, tiredness, less time for each other and conflicting parenting styles can combine to cause friction and isolation.

When families blend, children are present from the beginning, so many of the above factors are already at work. The kids are never far from the bedroom door, ready to intrude at any opportunity and many couples refrain from any sign of physical affection when children are within view (it can be unsettling for them, particularly when a relationship is new).

This is Petra's experience:

"There is never any time for us. Romance is not there any more. I thought I had the perfect relationship and for the most part we do, but when his kids came along, I then took my place at the back of the bus".

Petra

I've heard from many stepparents who believe their spouse places the needs of his or her children above their own. It causes them to resent their stepchildren and feel frustrated that their own needs are further down the list of priorities.

In God's natural order of creation, when a couple marry, they 'cleave' to each other. This basically means they're interdependent on each other to achieve more together than they can apart. After their relationship with God they make each other their main priority. Man and woman are joined together to take responsibility for each other's welfare and to love their mate above all others (Genesis, chpt 2 v 24). If parents meet each other's needs first and maintain a healthy relationship, this creates a loving and stable environment for children to be nurtured in.   When this natural order is changed or one person places work commitments, outsiders or children above their spouse's needs, breakdown begins.   We all know occasionally something in our lives takes more effort and energy, but if this basic order of priority is lost for a lengthy period of time, problems start.

This breakdown of priorities inevitably has a negative impact on children. You may have heard the saying "The best thing you can do for your child is to love their mother/father". This is not said to make you feel guilty about a previous relationship breakdown, but to guide you in successful future relationships.

See if you can relate to Margaret's comment:

"I feel that his priorities regarding finance, children are all geared towards his old relationship and nothing toward the new."

Margaret

Margaret isn't alone in feeling her needs are second best to her spouse's first wife. However, the natural order still remains; they must make it a priority to first consider each other's interests, so they can experience long-term fulfilment.

Note:
It is very important to make children your top priority after they have suffered the loss of a parent through death or divorce. They need plenty of time to grieve and adjust to their loss before placing them in a blended family environment. Only after you have made a marriage commitment should you consider each other's interests first in the decision making process **provided the safety or welfare of a child is never risked or compromised**. If you don't have a secure marriage relationship, you can't achieve a stable environment for children. This only sets them up to suffer another loss. Your children's needs still remain a top priority, but if your time and energies

are directed more towards meeting their needs instead of your partner's, you risk your relationship suffering as a consequence.

Say for example, you wanted some weekend time alone with your husband but he has access with his children every weekend and devotes the entire time to them so you're left on your own. Or, your wife decides to send her son to an expensive private school without considering your views. How would you feel? Chances are you wouldn't be jumping for joy! These kind of issues can and do cause resentment in relationships.

Again, I'm not saying that you have to neglect meeting your children's needs, but that you must take into consideration your spouse's needs. It's not about meeting the needs of your spouse at the expense of all else including children. It's about putting time and energy into developing a strong, loving and united front. This will provide your children with a secure environment. The goal is to achieve a balance between each area of your life so they work in harmony together, not as competing forces which cause you to feel continually torn.

Take time to ponder on the areas below and rate them on a scale, making number 1 your first priority to see where they currently lie (often how much time you devote to each one is a good indication of the order of importance). You may have others that you want to add and some may not feature in your life at all!

Friends	Work /income	Spiritual life
Children	Step-children	Extended family
Chores	Recreation/leisure	Voluntary service
Health – exercise	Spouse	Self-development (education)

Now we'll evaluate how satisfied you are with the order.

Is there balance between different areas or do a few tasks consume more than their **fair share** of time?

Are there areas you want to add to your life?

What motivates you for each area?

What level of personal satisfaction do you gain from each, i.e. little/average/a lot? (Chances are the higher the satisfaction, the higher the priority)

Whose needs does each of your top five priorities meet?

In what order would you like to see them?

What are the barriers to making your spouse your first priority?

What changes will you make?

To have a fulfilling relationship takes work, cooperation and time. Make time for your spouse a priority and discuss these issues.

One aim of this exercise is to give you the opportunity to reflect on how well balanced your life is. When we go through struggles, the problems themselves seem all-consuming and affect our enjoyment of everything else and life gets out of balance. Research supports the benefits of balance; for example, those who are prone to bouts of depression are less likely to experience future episodes if they exercise regularly, eat healthily and have 'time out' for themselves. The benefits of a balanced lifestyle are far reaching. By living a healthily balanced life, you pave the way to experience greater fulfilment in your relationship and set a positive example for your children.

Remember the strength of your marriage relationship forms the foundation upon which your blended family is built or broken. Before you can hope to resolve any challenge, you must work at establishing a healthy communication pattern. This is how you make each other a priority and begin the process:

Agree to discuss together all important decisions affecting your family. Take each other's thoughts and feelings into consideration when decisions arise, so you can act with your partner's interests in mind.

For stepparents this has an added benefit because you'll be less tempted to feel resentful that your needs are placed second to a child's, which is sometimes the case.

Now go through the following topics. They'll guide you towards using your time wisely to strengthen your relationship.

Strategy 2: Intimate Communication

People seldom struggle to chatter even if it's with someone they barely know. Often it may be a very general topic they speak on, like the weather. We may ask how a person is, or we are asked the same question. The typical response can vary between "Good" or "Fine" or "Well" or, "None of your business", depending on what kind of mood we're in. Regardless, we can be tempted to answer this question far from the truth. So why don't we just spill out how we really feel?

1. We know the person asking does so out of politeness, not necessarily genuine interest.

2. The environment or scene is not appropriate to go into detail.
3. We do not trust the person asking to understand or respect our feelings.
4. We fear that we will be rejected if we reveal our true self.

The four points above tell us that if we want to have intimate communication with someone we must therefore:

1. Take a genuine interest in them.
2. Create or wait for the right environment or setting, free from interruptions.
3. Have developed trust and rapport with the person.
4. Display an accepting and non-judgemental attitude.

When we communicate our thoughts and feelings to another, we become vulnerable. This can cause us to feel insecure if the person reacts in a manner we think condemns or rejects us. Here's an example: having just got a new hairstyle you ask your spouse whether it suits you. They reply, "Darling, with a face like yours, people aren't looking at your hair". Compliment or criticism? ☺ Well, it depends on the body language they used (more about this in Part 2).

To prevent people rejecting us, we often wear a 'mask' to protect ourselves. In other words, we try to act in a way we think will please others and make them like us. We hide our true feelings and self. However, communication with self disclosure is at the very heart of a relationship.

Self-disclosure draws others to us because it moves the relationship beyond a superficial acquaintance and allows us to be appreciated and understood for who we really are (don't you just get sick of only talking about the weather sometimes?). When we're real, it tends to draw others to us. Sharing our needs and failures releases us from the desire to hide behind a mask. I'm not advocating here that you spill your life history indiscriminately to everyone you meet (no, not everyone needs to know about what happened with the counsellor on the methadone program). More that meaningful relationships require openness and honesty. It takes time for trust to be gained, but often the benefits of an intimate relationship outweigh the necessary risk in becoming vulnerable. If smaller risks pay off, trust is gained so bigger risks can be taken towards self revelation.

Intimate communication is essential within a marriage if we are to remain in tune with our partner's wants and needs. The goal of intimate communication is to understand each other's thoughts, feelings, experiences and desires. It involves being open and honest and sharing from the heart. So if you want this kind of intimacy, here's some help…

Strategies to Encourage Intimate Communication:

- Set the scene: make time to talk where you will not be continually interrupted.

- Be open yourself: model the behaviour you want to encourage, it gives others the same freedom.

- Have time when you don't talk about work, children or the weather and use it to understand where each other is at on a personal level.

- Show respect for your partner's thoughts and feelings by encouraging them to express these: harsh judgments and criticisms will cause a person to clam up.

- Use reflective listening, for example "I hear you saying …."

- Empathise with their emotions, for example "You must feel hurt about this."

- Avoid interrupting or finishing your spouse's sentences.

- Avoid going off on a tangent.

- Let your body language show you are interested: nod, use eye contact and occasional touches.

- Show gratitude when your spouse confides in you; they may feel vulnerable to your rejection.

- Keep in confidence issues your spouse wants to remain only between the two of you.

You know you've listened well when the speaker believes you understand how they think and feel.

For some who struggle to express themselves verbally, a written letter can be a very powerful communicator. I have known people who find it very difficult to express their thought and feelings out loud, but on paper they can articulate themselves extremely well. If you are at point where verbal communication tends to be destructive, try writing a letter to your spouse. This can instigate a more intimate level of communication.

How much time do you currently spend each day talking about your thoughts, feelings and desires together?

Many couples do not have any specific plans to set aside quality time to enhance their relationship. If you fall into this category, try setting aside a specific time each day to catch up and communicate.

Strategy 3: Feeling and Showing Love

Often we do for our partner what we want them to do for us. We express our love in a way that would make us feel loved if they were to replicate the same behaviour. For example, one partner may shower their spouse with hugs and kisses (are you thinking "If only") or try to hold their hand when near because touch helps them feel loved. Their spouse, on the other hand, may not enjoy this but is frustrated when their partner won't make time to sit and talk with them.

No matter how well we know someone, we can't expect them to read our mind and behave in a way that lets us feel loved and appreciated. We must communicate with words as well as actions. The best thing you can do to be loved is to love others.

What have you done for your spouse in the past two weeks to make them feel loved?

What has your spouse done for you in the past two weeks that has caused you to feel loved?

Remember, we can't expect others to make us feel loved unless we **tell them** what they can do to help meet our needs. Write below what your partner can do for you to make you feel loved. Share your lists with each other.

But I don't feel like it!

If you're going through a difficult time in your relationship, you probably won't want to behave lovingly towards your spouse. Feelings and emotions will dictate your behaviour if you let them. However, if you want a fantastic relationship, you'll need to proactively make it happen. When the feeling of love is not there, choose to display a loving attitude. Yes, you can actually choose to let your feelings control your behaviour, or not. Here's an example:

Imagine a society where everyone both young and old had the attitude "If it feels good, do it".

How would my day look?
Well for a start, my children won't go to school because I know they don't 'feel' like it and I don't 'feel' like battling with them to make them go. I'll let my 9 year old son drive to the shops because he 'feels' that would be fun. I'm not going to cook dinner tonight (I hate cooking). The kids can go and help themselves to what ever they 'feel' like at the supermarket; in fact they don't even need to pay for their food if they don't 'feel' they want to. My stepson's made a huge mess in the garage and I sure don't 'feel' like being nice about that! I 'feel' like blasting him actually, so I guess that's what I'll do. First though, I think I'll go and have a coffee with that nice man down the road. He makes me 'feel' good about myself because he always has a compliment ready...

In our community and workplace we are governed by rules (laws) and expectations. As responsible adults we either abide by these, regardless of how we 'feel', or we risk the consequences (trouble with the law, loss of job, etc). What happens in our family though? There's no one to tell us we have to be nice or respectful regardless of how we 'feel'. Our family and relationships are one area of our life where we can behave as we 'feel'. So is it ok to let our 'feelings' govern our behaviour in these relationships? I love what Joyce Meyer (International Bible Teacher) has to say on this topic:

"Feelings change from day to day, hour to hour, even moment to moment. Not only do they change, they lie. You may be in a crowd of people and feel that everybody is talking about you, but that doesn't mean they are. You may feel that nobody understands you, but that doesn't mean they don't. If we want to be mature, disciplined people, we must be determined not to walk according to what we feel." (excerpt from "Who's the Boss, You or Your Emotions?" www.joycemeyer.org)

If we let our feelings rule our behaviour, we risk acting in our own interests, not in the best interests of those around us. If I blasted my stepson about the garage, it might make me temporarily 'feel' better but it would ultimately harm our relationship and certainly his respect for me. We all have the inborn tendency to be selfish or act in our own best interests. While it is important to acknowledge how we 'feel' when we're hurt or frustrated, after we've let it out we must let it go and move on for the sake of our relationships.

We can choose to behave in the best interests of our marriage. This decision, regardless of our circumstances, can ultimately enable us to experience a fulfilling relationship. We cannot control our spouse, but we can control our behaviour towards them. We do not need to let our emotions dictate our behaviour.

Here's what one woman told me about her experience:

"Our (now adult) children finally went their separate ways, leaving Jack and I to what was left of our marriage. All I kept thinking was that I had struggled for 22 years and it still hadn't made a difference, the bottom line was that we were

two separate and distinct families. I felt like the biggest failure. I didn't love him anymore and began to think of leaving. My deepest thoughts seemed to be constantly trying to figure out how and when I would leave. But I didn't.

After some time had passed I began wondering "Why am I still here"? Then I began to think about why we married in the first place. I thought back to the beginning and remembered telling my friends that we were getting married for all the right reasons. We had most things in common. We loved and enjoyed being with our children. We both worked in the same industry and always had plenty to talk about. We loved to travel, dance and have fun. We always enjoyed entertaining our friends and families, and I never really knew another guy who made me laugh the way he does. I came to the realization that "We are still a great couple". I feel that our commitment to the marriage enabled us to stay until we were able to find old feelings that we had buried away, but were certainly not gone. I know now that had I followed my feelings at the time and left, I would have regretted it."

When a relationship fails, sometimes it's because we 'feel' it's too hard to make it work. We have lost hope that it will get any better. Instead of believing the relationship can get better, hope is placed in life outside of the relationship. It can be tempting to think "Anything's got to be better than this!" Such thoughts breathe death into a relationship. In reality the relationship must have been good at some point or you wouldn't have committed yourself to your partner to begin with, right?

We've established that you will not always 'feel' love towards your spouse. So what can you do when you don't experience this feeling? Love becomes an action. Think back to what first attracted you to your spouse. Focus on their good qualities and act (behave) in a loving manner towards them. Encourage each other: "It's tough but we're going to get through this, it's going to get better!" So no matter how pessimistic you may be feeling right now, you can choose positive behaviour that will allow your feelings to follow. I have heard many cases where a person no longer 'feels' in love with their spouse, but has chosen to act in a loving manner. Amazingly enough, their feelings have followed the actions!

Try it and see for yourself. By the way, there is no "nice man down the road" ☺ but I hope you get the point.

Strategy 4: Appreciation and Encouragement

We all have the yearning to be loved and accepted for who we are, warts and all. However, our lives should not be based on continually seeking approval from others. We can never please everyone all the time. A person's approval or disapproval will only affect us if we let it and our spouse's attitude towards us can have the greatest impact.

Our spouse's acceptance or rejection of us has a powerful effect on our self worth. When we accept someone, we don't judge or try to change them. We can't change someone, no matter how much we would like to. We can only be responsible for our own actions. Acceptance doesn't mean we have to approve of a person's undesirable behaviour. For example, your spouse may do a bad thing but it doesn't mean they're a bad person; we still can love them as a person while disliking the behaviour. **We choose to focus on their good qualities**. Just as the words we speak over our children can have a powerful effect on their self-esteem, the same is true for our partner. With our words we hold the power to either tear them down, or build them up. Our words will directly affect our spouse's self image so it is important we choose them carefully.

Have you ever told your spouse you both **want** and **need** them in your life? To admit that we need someone is to confess we feel inadequate without them. Letting our spouse know we need them gives them a sense of purpose within the marriage. It allows them to feel satisfaction through their usefulness. I read in one survey that 70% of people leave their jobs because they don't feel valued? We all want to be appreciated. We all take delight in feeling wanted and needed by those around us. This is in line with God's intention for marriage; that we achieve more together as a couple, than we can apart.

A key to effective encouragement is its genuineness.

There is no point in encouraging someone if you're not being honest or not basing your encouragement on a specific quality.

Everyone has their own strengths and weaknesses. It is our areas of strength that we most enjoy being complimented on. I've listed some areas:

- ✓ Organisation and administration ability
- ✓ Giving praise and encouragement to others
- ✓ Showing compassion and mercy
- ✓ Training and teaching others
- ✓ Giving generously of possessions and money and gifts
- ✓ Showing hospitality and entertaining others
- ✓ Offering wisdom and guidance and insight
- ✓ Artistic, musical, performing and sporting abilities

If we are particularly good at something, we gain a sense of achievement when people notice. I was speaking with someone recently who said he told his partner what a hard worker he thought she was. He said her face just lit up, it was like she'd won a million dollars. Because work was important to her, she greatly valued his compliment. Had he complimented her on something that wasn't important to her, such as her clothes, the compliment would not have had such a powerful effect. Encouragement becomes meaningful when based on a specific quality we value.

You will see that I have listed the quality of praise and encouragement as a strength. Some people seem to be naturally gifted at encouraging others. They use their words to uplift others by dwelling on the good they bring to a situation. A positive attitude and the ability to encourage make a person fun to be around. This combined with honesty about one's own shortcomings conveys a sense of acceptance for others' weaknesses and fosters intimate friendships.

There will be things that your partner feels are important which you don't (my husband's never too impressed with me if I don't drool over his new car). Taking an interest in what matters to your spouse lets them know you care. Have another look at your spouse's list on Strategy 3 as a reminder of how you can make them feel loved and appreciated this week. Below are further discussion points for you to share, specifically geared towards expressing appreciation:

1. What is one thing I am really pleased my spouse does well?
2. What is something I admire which my spouse has done or made?
3. What do I like about my spouse's appearance?
4. What is the quality I most value in my spouse?

One of the deepest purposes of marriage is to encourage one another to reach their fullest potential.

A marriage should not restrict the freedom of either spouse to fulfil their individual destinies. To this degree, each person requires independence within the relationship. A husband and wife can be united with delight and pride as they watch each other grow and develop as a person.

What activity is my spouse passionate about or do they enjoy the most?

What are my husband's/wife's long-term goals/dreams/ambitions, or what do they hope to achieve before they die?

What can I do to help/support them to achieve this?

Ask the same questions of yourself and identify what it is you would like your spouse to do to support you.

Strategy 5: Overcome the Barriers to Intimacy

Manipulation

Manipulation means deviously controlling a situation to benefit your self. It is destructive to relationships. People who use manipulative behaviour tend to do so in one of three ways.

Firstly, there's the 'I'm in control' person who likes to make all the practical decisions and insists on having their own way. These people enjoy correcting and belittling others, and feel the need to prove they know more about a topic being discussed than anyone else.

The second type of manipulation comes about through the 'poor me' attitude. This person may spend hours talking about their own problems and tends to cling to others. They may unconsciously dwell on or use their problems as an excuse to ensure people stay by them.

The third type of manipulation occurs when a person finds it 'necessary to be needed'. They are happiest when someone needs help and they are there to assist. Unfortunately this behaviour can encourage the dependency of those receiving the help.

Here's an example of the 'I'm in control' manipulation. It illustrates how this barrier to intimacy can destroy a relationship:

"What can I do to get Glen to compromise and be kinder to me and my children? Although Glen has married me, he threatens to leave regularly. What should I do about this, if anything? How much 'giving in' is too much for me?"

Liz

Liz is compromising by sacrificing her own values or needs and those of her children's in order to keep the peace. Glen's threats to leave are a form of manipulation; he has discovered he can get his own way by using this unhealthy behaviour. These threats create uncertainty and instability for everyone involved. To prevent Liz's growing resentment she needs be strong in defining her own boundaries or limits on a particular issue and communicate these to Glen. To have a healthy relationship both parties' views must be accounted for in decision-making. If she calls his bluff on leaving, by not giving in completely but standing her ground, he will no longer be able to use the threat as manipulation.

To help you identify ways you might try to manipulate others, ask yourself the following:

1. Do I tend to be happy only when I have my own way in decision making?
2. Do I like to be in control of other's behaviour?
3. Do I use my problems to gain attention and sympathy from others?
4. Am I mostly interested in relationships where people depend on me for assistance?

If you answered, "Yes" to any of the above, have a look at why you manipulate others.

What beliefs contribute to this behaviour and prevent you from accepting personal responsibility?

What new thinking and behaviour could you use instead to overcome manipulation?

Give your spouse permission to point out when you're falling back into old patterns.

Dishonesty & Criticism

Strict truthfulness is generally not expected in social circles. It's not uncommon for people to tell little 'white lies' as a convenience and to avoid hurting other's feelings ("No, that doesn't make your bum look big dear"). However in a marriage relationship, a couple must trust each other to speak truthfully if they are to experience intimacy. Once a husband or wife begins to lie either by positive deception, or withholding the truth, breakdown can begin. If one partner feels there is no longer complete openness between them or one's word can't be trusted, suspicion starts to breed, and resentment can soon follow. Honesty is therefore the best policy, but truth must always be spoken in love with the other person's best interests at heart. This requires diplomacy and tact. In other words, don't go saying "Well, if you're comparing your bum to an elephant's, then no".

There is a time and a place for constructive criticism – this is covered more in Part 2. For now it is sufficient to say you should be slow to point out negatives and do so only after carefully deliberating your motive. If you find yourself enjoying criticising another, chances are your motives are not right. It may be that you are doing it to make yourself look good. If you find it difficult or painful to do, it is more likely that your intentions are not for your own good, but to genuinely help the other overcome a problem.

How important to me is my spouse's honesty?

Do I strive to be completely honest with my spouse?

On what occasions or under what circumstances do I lie to my spouse?

If I lie to my spouse, what is my motive for doing so?

Does my spouse expect complete honesty from me?

Looking at your answers, is there anything you need to change to progress further towards a healthy relationship?

Dishonesty drains a relationship of intimacy. Respectful honesty produces a healthy, fulfilling relationship. The best way to encourage trustworthiness is to trust someone conversely, to make someone untrustworthy, don't trust them! I came across this quote recently:

"The person who trusts others will always lose less than the person who distrusts them"

Jealousy

In a marriage relationship, we naturally want to protect the love and affection we have for each other to keep it exclusively our own. This desire for exclusive intimacy protects the sanctity of marriage. It is therefore healthy and natural to resent the threat of invasion.

If one partner feels threatened by outside influences on the relationship, despite conclusive proof their fears are unnecessary, it can be said they are experiencing irrational jealously. In extreme cases this can become an emotional illness if it does not yield to 'common-sense'. Jealousy can sometimes be the symptom of emotional insecurity; one partner may feel they are not good enough for the other. In this case the insecurity is not based on fact but on a person's own self-worth. A relationship is only as healthy as the two people who comprise it.

To expect one person alone to meet all our needs is to put an enormous and unrealistic pressure on our relationship. Our marriage partner should be our best friend, but not our only friend. To overcome destructive feelings of jealously we need to recognise where jealousy comes from and its root cause. If we want our partner to be solely dependent on us to meet their needs and vice versa, we will overcrowd them and each end up dissatisfied. We are enriched through our relationships with others and our interests outside of the relationship. We can overcome jealously in our adult relationships by developing other healthy friendships and activities.

I often receive the following comment from stepmothers and fathers:

"I find myself feeling very jealous of my stepchildren's relationship with my partner".

Mark

A stepparent's jealousy often comes as a result of feeling their needs are placed second best to the child's. Jealously is a very real and powerful emotion. The jealously here, if left unchecked, could affect the marriage relationship and the stepparent/child relationship through strong feelings of resentment. This reaction is quite natural if the partner's priority is their own children, and not their spouse.

To overcome jealousy, stepparents must communicate their feelings to their partner in a sensitive manner. I am not suggesting a parent sacrifice meeting their children's needs to meet those of their partner, but rather that they work together so everyone feels satisfied. It is possible but may require some 'give and take'. This goes back to the earlier point about taking each other's thoughts and feelings into consideration when decisions arise, so you can act with your partner's interests in mind.

Have a look at the following questions to assess whether the issue of jealously is harming your relationship:

On what occasions do I feel jealous regarding my spouse's priorities or affections?

What is the basis for my jealously?

Do my feelings of jealously negatively affect our relationship?

What would I need my spouse to do or say to make me feel more confident and secure within our relationship?

One final question:

What can I do right now for my husband/wife to improve our marriage?

In Summary

We have talked about successful marriages requiring work. The main key to a healthy relationship is the commitment to make each other a priority by setting aside quality time to communicate and enjoy each other. I remember the following comment from someone who had recently gone through a divorce:

"I would look around me at all the other couples I knew, thinking they were happily married, and often wondered what the heck was wrong with me or my marriage – why weren't we like all those others."

What this person failed to realize was that every one of those 'other couples' has and will continue to have issues that cause friction but, as long as they are prepared to work at resolving them in a healthy manner, they will stay married successfully.

I recently read that American researchers have discovered many people pursue a permanent state of happiness in their family relationships, like the fairytales where everyone lives 'happily ever after'. Unfortunately this is very destructive to family life. Why? Because true domestic bliss (without suffering) is not possible despite what the fairy tales tell us.

If we give up every time the going gets tough, we will never get the chance to experience the joy of a successful long-term relationship. While a permanent state of happiness cannot be achieved, families can work together through the good and bad times. So it's not the absence of conflict that makes a healthy family, but the ability to resolve it in a positive manner – we'll look at this shortly.

So what does this mean for you and me? Accept that in your family there will be both high and low times. Successful marriages are those that value grace and forgiveness. They stay committed even when the 'feeling' of love is not there and work to resolve issues through the tough times they invariably face.

You need to believe your marriage is worth working on and be committed to success before you'll achieve it. Be encouraged, you can have a great marriage if you both expect and plan for it!

"Continuous effort, not strength or intelligence, is the key to unlocking our potential."

Winston Churchill

Part Two

~~~~~~~~~~~~

Resolving
Conflict

"The ability to speak several languages is an asset, but the ability to keep your mouth shut in one language is priceless."

Ancient Proverb

Conflict is a part of life because we are unique individuals. Two people will never agree on everything all the time. We know statistically that more second marriages fail than first marriages. To succeed, we need skills for resolving conflict. Most of these skills are ideally taught from a young age in the home environment; sometimes this is not the case. Some couples never resolve conflict, so issues get ignored for a while only to eventually resurface. This can cause an invisible wall of resentment to build which reduces intimacy and affects the emotional health of the couple. A couple's ability to resolve conflict directly affects the health of their relationship, so this part will equip you with strategies for resolving conflict.

Conflict isn't bad. It is a normal and healthy part of life. I say healthy because no two people can possibly think alike all the time. Our spouse will have different opinions to our own. It would be wrong to suppress our own thoughts and opinions in a relationship for the sake of keeping the peace. Everyone has the right to express his or her own views. It is wise for a couple to openly address their differences rather than conceal their resentments.

The goal of all conflict in a relationship should be "To mutually negotiate and agree upon the outcome".

Left unresolved, conflict can destroy a relationship as each person becomes increasingly dissatisfied and distant from the other. So how can we work towards healthy resolution? I'll show you!

Strategy 1: Experiences of Conflict

Our first experience of conflict comes from our childhood home. We observe the way the adults around us handle conflict. This sets a foundation for our attitude towards conflict and the way we approach it. We also experience conflict first hand with our siblings and peers. I have spoken with some people who say they never saw their parents argue. This unfortunately means they also never saw how to effectively work through and resolve points of difference. They, along with those who witnessed a lot of disunity without reconciliation, may have missed out on seeing successful keys to healthy relationships such as taking responsibility for one's own actions, apologising and seeing forgiveness in action. Take the opportunity now to look at how your experiences have shaped your approach to conflict.

When I was a child how did the adults in my life resolve conflict?

What are my earliest memories of conflict with others and how was it handled?

What strategies towards conflict have I learned from those around me?

What is my impression of conflict now as an adult; is it a good or bad thing?

Was conflict successfully resolved in any previous relationships? If not, what could **I** have done differently?

Some people are constantly on the defensive and pointing their finger at another. If a person is willing to take responsibility for their own actions by apologising when in the wrong, it can help defuse tension in a relationship. If a couple has respect for each other, they have a greater chance of resolving conflict in a healthy manner. If one person is more preoccupied in meeting his or her own needs, conflict is more likely to be destructive to the relationship.

The following questions are designed to give you an indication of your ability to resolve conflict in a healthy manner.

1. Do I repeatedly go over old hurts?

2. Do I accept responsibility for my actions – right and wrong?

3. Do I forgive (not bear a grudge against another) when wronged?

4. Am I honest in telling my spouse how I feel?

5. Are there times when I keep quite to 'keep the peace' in this relationship?

6. Do I listen to my partner's concerns?

7. Am I able to empathise with my partner's point of view?

8. How flexible am I on issues I feel strongly about; do I compromise easily?

9. Do I think my partner tries to understand my views and feelings?

When conflict arises in your current relationship, what motivates you to respond in your most usual manner? Here are some usual responses:

- Hopelessness; unless I give in, we will continue fighting.
- Control; the need to have my own way because I know best.
- Respect; to consider each other's needs before agreeing on a solution.
- Fear of confrontation; the need to maintain peace at any cost.
- Have my say: the desire to express strong emotions and words.

Addressing our own experiences and approach to conflict helps us identify learned behaviour and understand why we find ourselves reacting the way we do. We can then see what changes we need to make to work towards healthy resolution.

Conflict involves at least two parties, however we only have control over one party; ourself! We are powerless to change another person's behaviour but we can change our own. Healthy resolution therefore begins with getting our own approach and attitude to conflict right. If we find ourselves reacting harshly to a situation by yelling for example, we encourage others to retaliate in a similar manner. Conversely, we can choose to show respect through listening and reflection. This in turn helps defuse tension in a situation and models the behaviour we want to see in others.

Take a look at your answers to the questions in this section. Highlight any problem areas you feel would be most beneficial for you to address. The information here will give you new ways of resolving conflict. At the end of Part 2, come back to the highlighted issues and reflect on how and when you can put actions in place to overcome them using the guidelines given.

Strategy 2: Conflict Styles

The aim of this strategy is to look at how you commonly approach conflict, to examine your motive for using a particular style and to identify appropriate settings for each style.

Dr James Fairfield, famous for his work identifying conflict styles, has suggested the following five approaches to conflict:

1. **Yield**: You give in to keep the peace and save the relationship but fail to meet the goals of it.

2. **Withdraw**: Avoid confrontation by removing yourself physically or psychologically from the situation; it can mean giving up on the relationship, or withdrawing temporarily to cool off.

3. **Win**: You dominate to have your own way. You look after your own interests which may be at the cost of the relationship.

4. **Compromise**: You give in to some of the other's demands, making the same request of them; this can work for some issues but the bargaining may cause you to have to sacrifice your own needs or values.

5. **Resolve**: You use open and direct communication to change a situation, attitude or behaviour.

It may be appropriate to use any one of these styles depending on the situation for example, you may choose to:

Yield: It might be necessary to give in for a time if you are forced into a win-lose situation until an appropriate opportunity arises to resolve the disagreement.

Withdraw: Appropriate if emotions are strong and you need to calm down for a period.

Win: Could be used when a decision must be made immediately after consulting with the other.

Compromise: Used where no agreement can be made other than by each person negotiating, or giving in on some aspects to reach a mutually acceptable decision.

Resolve: Used where each other's thoughts and feelings on an issue can be explored and understood to come to a consensus about the most appropriate course of action.

Which style of resolution do you mostly use?

Which style does your spouse mostly use?

People who struggle to resolve conflict can find themselves responding to conflict in one of two ways: they're either a ……

1. **Bull**
   - Rushes head on into conflict
   - Confrontational
   - Attacks verbally when provoked

…or a…

2. *Hedgehog*
   - Retreats when confronted
   - Avoids conflict to keep the peace
   - Not verbally responsive, tend to clam up

Both of these responses avoid dealing with the issue because energy is directed towards either attacking each other or avoiding each other. For the issue to be resolved it must be separated from the relationship and dealt with. The following diagram best illustrates the point.

ME ------------- ISSUE ------------- **SPOUSE**

The issue in this case, creates a rift that separates the couple from each other. For healthy conflict resolution to occur, **a couple must recognise they both share the same ultimate goal of wanting to resolve the conflict and enjoy an intimate relationship**. They are both on the same team working together to tackle the conflict. The issue must remain separate from their relationship as below.

ME ------------- ISSUE
SPOUSE

Identify your tendency to avoid or attack (be a bull or hedgehog). This is an area of weakness you will need to consciously work to overcome when you use the principles outlined in the rest of this part.

During disagreements do we deal with the issue, avoid or attack each other?

Here's an example of how an ineffective conflict pattern can destroy a relationship:

"Warren is a wonderful caring person. He is excellent in so many avenues. The thing I find sad is the demise of our relationship through his confrontational attitude. The minute anyone disagrees with him, I am sure he looks at it as a challenge that he has to win. I am unsure whether to continue long-term in this relationship."

Sally

It is clear the inability to resolve conflict is contributing to the relationship breakdown and could very well destroy it. The issues need to be addressed with a united approach to resolving the **source** of conflict, not placing the conflict as a barrier between them.

Skills to Use During Conflict:

- Concentrate on the facts and don't judge motives.

- Keep contributing 'behaviour' separate from the character of a person. For example, a comment like, "You're so selfish, you always have to win" attacks a person's character.

- You're on the same team; tackle the issue, not each other (except maybe when making up!!).

Strategy 3: Listening

I just love this quote so I am going to repeat it:

> *"The ability to speak several languages is an asset, but the ability to keep your mouth shut in one language is priceless."*

The expression "We are given two ears but only one mouth; we should listen a lot more than we talk" is a good guideline. The ability to both listen and reflect back to the speaker what we've heard, are communication skills that may not come naturally but can be learned. Listening is not about letting the other person talk while we are thinking of our own response. The purpose of listening is to gain an **understanding** of another's thoughts, feelings and opinions. We need to appreciate the situation from their perspective or point of view.

We all have the potential to interpret information differently, according to our own agenda. This means the message a person is trying to get across may not be what we hear. Sometimes we may find ourselves guilty of selective listening or only picking up on cues that confirm our own way of thinking. If we don't like what is being said or the tone of voice, we may shut off or focus on our own reactions and miss the real meaning. Effective listening requires effort on our part. It shows respect for the other's views and feelings.

"...be quick to listen, slow to speak and slow to get angry."

James 1v19

How to Develop Effective Listening Skills:

- Concentrate on the words.
- Do not let your mind be distracted by your own thoughts of response.
- Accept without judgment what is being said.
- Don't interrupt (my husband tells me it's frustrating ☺).
- Be open to the other's suggestions; don't shut them down with criticisms.
- Look at body language; can you tell how a person is feeling by watching them?
- Maintain comfortable eye contact.
- Use your own body language to show interest; lean towards the person with relaxed posture.
- Sit or stand on the same level.
- Avoid distracting behaviour such as fidgeting (and no more rapping fingers on the table).
- Pay attention to what is being said.
- Show genuine interest.

To identify how well we have achieved this we should:

1. **Repeat what we have heard the person say** (try using their words)
2. **Identify how they felt when they were speaking**

This is called reflective listening.

We need to accept or understand what the other feels without judgment if we want to encourage intimate communication. If you and your spouse struggle in this area, try the following suggestion:

1. Get a set of keys (or similar). The person holding the keys is the only one allowed to talk.

2. The first person with the keys can talk for up to 2 minutes before handing the keys over to the other.

3. The second person must reflect back what they heard the first person say and how they think the person was feeling. Next, hand the keys back to the first person.

4. The first person then responds with how well they felt they were heard.

5. Now the second person takes 2 minutes to have their say holding the keys while the other listens. The cycle repeats until both feel heard and understood.

The keys are used to avoid the other interrupting until it's their turn to speak. Take a look at the following questions to evaluate what you can do to improve in this area.

Can you and your partner express your thoughts and feelings during conflict?

Do you try to understand each other's views?

Using the above guidelines, what will you do to listen more effectively to each other?

Strategy 4: How to Avoid Criticism

Three common reasons people fall into the trap of criticising a person are:

1. To vent their frustration with a particular behaviour.

2. To build themselves up or feel more important: it can help them feel better if someone else looks bad.

3. They may have personally experienced a lot criticism so it has become a learned behaviour.

Regardless of these reasons, criticism serves to alienate others. This strategy will show you how to make a positive request in place of nagging criticisms.

Before confronting others with what we believe are their faults, we must first examine our own motives and attitudes. Failure to do this and to speak the truth with love will cause division. No one is perfect but we all have a tendency to expect perfection in others, particularly our spouse and children or stepchildren. This inevitably causes disappointment. In a relationship based on respect, we don't have the right to be critical, but we do have the right to speak the truth with love and compassion. Often our spouse may be the only person in our life to confront us with personal issues or wrong motives that we need to address such as anger, resentments or guilt driven behaviour. If our motive for requesting a change is to genuinely help the other overcome a problem for their personal benefit, we are on the right track.

Do I find myself being critical often?

What is my motive for criticising my spouse?

Continual criticism will drive a couple apart. Encouragement breathes life into relationships and criticism brings death. In a relationship we need to know we are loved and accepted despite our faults. The goal is to know everything about each other yet love and respect each other just the same. **Part of a great marriage is building each other's self worth and growing together through communication.**

The following strategies will help you avoid criticism.

1. Don't get defensive

Our natural tendency when faced with criticism is to become defensive. When we choose to act defensively, our goal becomes to justify our behaviour to preserve our sense of self worth. When we feel we're being personally attacked it's natural to want to defend ourselves. Using phrases like the following, automatically make us want to justify our self and retaliate back:

"Why did you do that?"
or
"How can you say that?"
or
"What made you do that?"

This form of questioning (or interrogation) is like pointing the finger at someone while demanding an explanation. Discuss with your partner other less threatening options. Try phrasing questions along the following lines:

"I'd like to know how you feel about this."
or
"Help me understand what caused that to happen."
or
"Tell me what you were thinking when this happened."

Why do I defend my own behaviour?

What can I change so I no longer act defensively or encourage my spouse to?

Remember, it is two people's differences that cause conflict. If we take responsibility for our own contribution to a problem, it shows a willingness to cooperate and encourages the other to be more open to discussion.

2. Compliment instead of condemn

Our words have the power to either tear others down or build them up. The power they have can be likened to the rudder of a huge ship. In comparison to the size of a ship, the rudder is a small part, yet it has the power to steer the direction of the ship in adverse conditions and against strong winds. Our words have the same effect in steering us down the path to destructive relationships or to edify, encourage and bring out the best in others. We must use them carefully.

People respond far more favourably to encouragement than to criticism. If we tell someone often enough that they're no good or can't be trusted, chances are they'll continue to confirm our words. For example, if your partner has an office function on one evening and you say to him/her "I know I can't trust you to come home sober, you always have too much too drink when you're with your work colleagues", they'll probably live up to your expectations. If instead you say "Darling I'd love to spend some quality time with you tonight, I know you're reliable and I can trust you to stay sober so we can enjoy some time together when you get home", there's greater likelihood they won't disappoint you.

When we are motivated to speak from our negative emotions, we may tend to complain or nag. We can make a positive request in a kind manner instead of criticising the other for their behaviour. For example, instead of saying "I'm sick of telling you to stop yelling" try, "I really want to hear what you have to say, could you please lower your voice so we can discuss why you are angry."

Encouragement searches for the best in others and brings it to light:

"I saw an angel in the marble and carved until I set him free"
Michaelangelo

I recently heard on the radio some medical research that now recognises the power that words can have over one's physical health. Just as feeding ourselves psychological messages such as "I'm useless" can act as a self-fulfilling prophecy causing us to fail, the same is true for our physical well being. Those who remain optimistic about their health may experience fewer long-term problems. How about that!

"Kind words are like honey - sweet to the soul and healthy for the body"

Proverbs 16v24

How many compliments do you give your spouse each day compared to criticisms?

3. Request rather than demand

While we can't make or demand another person change, we can lovingly request they change their behaviour if it's destructive to the health of our family life. People are often a lot more responsive to a positive request for change if it comes along side words of encouragement. For example:

"You mean the world to me, Joe. When you criticise me in front of the children I feel belittled and angry with you. Do you feel this is something you can change because I love you very much and want the best for our relationship?"

People can resent being told what to do or bossed about. Giving an order such as "Go and spend some time with Ollie," cuts off communication and gives no opportunity for response. **Orders make people feel like the behaviour is expected, rather than appreciated.**   People who respond to an order are more likely to feel resentful because their own view or commitment to do the task is not taken into consideration. They are also liable to feel unappreciated. Suggestions such as those used in the following phrases can evoke a more favourable response:

- "Would you like to spend some time with Ollie so I can just get this done? He'd love the attention."
- "You are so good with Ollie, is it possible for you to go and play with him?"
- "What do you think about spending some time with Ollie while I'm busy here? It would mean a lot and I'd really appreciated it."

The following questions will help you recognise destructive behaviour and work towards positive change.

What do **you** do that causes your spouse to be angry or frustrated with you?

For you to change this behaviour, what needs to happen?

How can your spouse encourage you to achieve the change?

What does **your spouse** do that causes the most anger and frustration in you?

What can your spouse do to change their behaviour pattern?

(Remember to make a positive request, e.g. it would really benefit everyone if we could decide on a consistent approach to discipline.)

How can you encourage your spouse achieve the change?

Strategy 7 outlines 6 steps to resolving conflict. At the end of Part 2, come back to these questions and together use the steps to help you resolve your issues. Reflect on the suggested behaviour change and explain how you feel about the request. Apologise for any wrongdoing on your part and find a solution you both agree upon.

Write here the solutions you have agreed to put into practice.

Strategy 5: The Power of Emotions!

The two factors common to every disagreement are a difference of opinion and the emotional heat attached to the difference. Our emotions may be perfectly justifiable but they need to be managed and not expressed blindly. By working quickly towards resolving conflict, we can starve our negative emotions.

There are 3 parts to communication: words, voice tone and body language. Most often the actual content or words make up a only small part of the message people receive when we speak. Often our emotions are expressed through our body language and voice tone. **It's not what is being said, but the way it is being said that can have the most impact**.

If the three parts of communication contradict each other a person receives a confusing message. For example, a person says to their spouse "Darling would you be able to do this job for me?". The response back might be "Yes, once I've finished up here". This could be said either in a cheerful tone with a head nod to convey a willing compliance with the request, or the same words could be said in a tired, frustrated tone with a side shake of the head, implying it's the last thing on earth they feel like doing. Body language therefore needs to be interpreted alongside the words spoken to understand the message a person is sending.

To avoid confusion we need to share our feelings honestly and align our body language with the message we are sending. Our spouse is then not left having to second-guess our meaning when we speak.

Negative emotions are a natural part of life. To have an intimate relationship we must give each other permission to express them. We cannot possibly feel "happy" all the time. Sometimes due to stress, tiredness or hormones we get grumpy. We need the security of knowing we will not be rejected if we're having a bad day and feeling low. Our emotions can be totally unrelated to anything our spouse has done. Sometimes we just need to verbalise this to avoid offending them:

"Honey, I've had a rough day and I'm feeling tired. I'm not snapping at you because of anything you've done wrong, I'm just a bit low."

When our spouse does something to offend us, or fails to do what we believe they should have done, it arouses negative emotions in us. **While feeling these emotions may be natural and beyond our control, we can control how we express them.** If we react negatively to the situation using accusations and hurtful words, we can expect a negative reaction in return. We can choose to speak kindly despite our negative feelings.

Possibly one of the most powerful emotions we experience is that of anger. **If your emotions are very strong, withdraw from a situation until they have settled down.** It is worth waiting a few hours to resolve the issue as strong emotions like anger can drive you apart.

"I was angry, for I had no shoes. Then I met a man who had no feet."
Chinese proverb

The root of anger lies in hurt, fear and frustration. Anger is the trigger for violence and verbal abuse. If issues are left unresolved, anger can build to eventually blow up when it is finally expressed. In its heat, anger will prevent you from approaching a situation objectively.

Unfair Weapons of Warfare!

- Belittling the other's opinions and feelings
- Silent treatment
- Dishonesty
- Violence
- Verbal abuse
- Sarcasm

How do you both react when you are angry?

It is commonly recommended that when we want to express our dissatisfaction at another person's actions, we do so using "I" statements. For example:

"**I** feel angry when this happens"
Or
"When you say that, it makes **me** feel that you don't love me"

The person speaking is taking ownership of their feelings. Focus is on the individual's own response to the other person's behaviour. Remember to **focus on the behaviour, not the character** of a person. You still love them; it's their behaviour that's contributing to the problem.

While it is true that another's behaviour can trigger an immediate emotional reaction in us, sometimes we can have the same emotions by failing to guard our thought process. Negative thoughts evoke negative feelings. **We can pamper our negative feelings by dwelling on the bad points we see in others.** A word of caution: if a person is continually telling their spouse that they feel hurt, angry, disappointed, etc. by their spouse's actions, the spouse will end up feeling a complete failure. **I am not saying we should deny our negative emotions but neither should we feed them.** Remember the section on compliments? We should place our energies into bringing out the best in others and role model the behaviour we want to see in them.   Before expressing negative emotions ask yourself what you hope to achieve.

When we are confronted with another's feelings, we can respond in one of two ways. For example:

Peter says to Lisa: *"I feel you don't like my son Johnny."*
Lisa responds: *"You are so mean; look at all I do for him."*

This response condemns Peter's feelings and may start a war.

If Lisa responds with *"What causes you to feel this way?"*, she accepts his feelings and keeps the lines of communication open.

Another quick tip - **don't use broad generalisations** such as "You always" or "You never". Apart from causing the recipient to feel attacked, they are seldom true!

How to Keep Emotions Under Control:
- ✓ Tell how the behaviour makes you feel
- ✓ Don't let your mind dwell on the negative but actively focus on the positive
- ✓ Work quickly to resolve conflict
- ✓ Stick to the issue; do not generalize
- ✓ Accept your spouse's negative feelings
- ✓ Ensure your body language is consistent with your message

Looking at the guidelines, what will you commit to doing to express your emotions in a healthy manner?

"A truly wise person uses few words; a person with understanding is even-tempered. Even fools are thought to be wise when they keep silent; when they keep their mouths shut, they seem intelligent."
Proverbs 17 v27 28   ☺

Strategy 6: Overcoming Past Hurts

No one is perfect, so it's impossible to completely avoid hurting our spouse, or being hurt by them. The hurt may happen unintentionally through words, actions or inaction. When hurt we may react with anger, want to retaliate, feel resentful or lose trust in a person. When hurts are not resolved in a marriage, they manifest and grow into a wall of resentment which inhibits communication. When couples stop trusting each enough to share their thoughts and feelings, they can become emotionally separate.

"Love your neighbour as yourself. But instead of showing love among yourselves you are always biting and devouring one another, watch out! Beware of destroying one another."

Galatians 5v14 15

We must be careful not to allow resentment to turn into bitterness which destroys each other and the relationship. The following confession from Becky illustrates how this can potentially happen:

"On occasions I feel he favours his children in certain issues but I don't know what to do about it. His favouritism makes me feel less important. I found that my partner was doing extra things for his daughter that I didn't know about and now I feel I am the one that has to get pass this jealously but I don't know how. It is tearing me up inside. He manages to get the time off for his own family but always seems to be unable to when it is for my family. This hurts me and again I feel less important which contributes to my feelings of insecurity."

Becky

Becky identifies three areas of discontent that are not resolved. Each behaviour reinforces her feelings of neglect and increases her dissatisfaction. Until these are addressed, Becky's husband will continue to unwittingly confirm her insecurities: his favouritism is reinforced in her mind by his willingness to take time off work for his children but not her own. Each issue needs to be worked through separately to tear down this wall and prevent increasing resentment towards her husband and his children. We've covered the topic of prioritising our spouse's needs, and it is my opinion that Becky feels insecure because her husband's dishonesty and use of time causes her to feel her thoughts/needs are not a priority.

Enough about Becky, now we'll focus on you.

How have I caused my spouse to feel hurt in our relationship?

How have I been hurt in our relationship?

Have these hurts been resolved or built walls of resentment in our relationship?

When we admit our mistakes and ask for our spouse's help, we stop building walls and make existing ones easier to demolish. Confession and forgiveness are integral to destroying walls.

Whatever the hurt, it is necessary for the person in the wrong to repent of their actions before restoration can take place. This repentance allows them to directly receive forgiveness. It is only through forgiveness that the marriage relationship can be healed and restored. So what does it mean to repent?

True repentance includes recognising the pain our wrong actions have caused and endeavouring never to repeat the offending behaviour. It does not seek to justify the behaviour or blame it on anyone or anything but takes responsibility for it. To help our spouse to move beyond the hurt we have caused them, we must apologise and ask for their forgiveness.

Here is an example of an apology that accepts responsibility for the wrong action:

"I am sorry I did that, it was wrong of me"

Not:

"If you hadn't said what you did, I wouldn't have done that", this blames the behaviour on the other person.

To Summarise:
1. Confess wrongdoing
2. Take responsibility for the behaviour
3. Ask for forgiveness
4. Determine never to repeat the behaviour

I could add "Seek to repay or make up for the wrong doing", which may be appropriate in criminal matters, but in a marriage the best action is to commit wholeheartedly to grow in love together. To forgive someone requires us to release him or her from the burden of guilt they feel so they do not continually try and "make-it-up" to us, motivated by their guilt. **We need our spouse's affirmation and support to be based on their love for us, not the guilt they experience as a consequence of their own wrongdoing.**

Forgiveness is for our benefit, to release us from bitterness. It is a choice, not a feeling. **Forgiveness brings healing and reconciliation to a marriage relationship**. It is the continual process of choosing not to harbour resentments towards the other by bringing up the past. It is the day-by-day choice to let the past go that will gradually lead to wholeness.

Tips on Forgiveness:

- Forgiveness is not a feeling; if you wait for your feelings to change, they may never.

- **Forgiveness is an attitude that requires action**. Choose to let go of the pain someone has caused you by not dwelling on the offence.

- When you choose to forgive, your mind may be tempted to relive old hurts over again. Take control over your thoughts, leave the past alone (it can never change), and focus solving the current issues.

- If your attitude and behaviour are negative towards a person, you can expect a negative response in return; fill your mind with positive thoughts - you need to think positively before you will be able to act positively.

We can still practice the principle of forgiveness when our spouse has not apologised. If we hold on to anger and resentments they have the potential to destroy both the relationship and ourselves. Feelings of love can also be destroyed if one person in a relationship continually refuses to apologise for their own wrongdoing. The reality is, some people find it incredibly easy to point their finger in blame without looking at their own imperfections.

I know of couples who have gone for years with one partner refusing to apologise for anything they have done wrong. Does this mean that this person was not to blame at all in any conflict? Of course not! Sometimes people refuse to accept how their own actions or attitudes contribute to a situation. In one case a woman (Anne) gave her husband the silent treatment while acting self-righteous for days after he had done something unintentional to upset her. She couldn't understand why he became angry towards her because, in Anne's mind, she was the one wronged. Anne's silent treatment caused her husband to feel hurt and resentful because he was not allowed the opportunity to discuss the issue and put things right. In this particular scenario, to resolve the conflict Anne must also seek her husband's forgiveness for her self-righteous attitude.

We should not consider ourselves better than anyone else but seek to respond with love and compassion when we are hurt, just as we would want others to respond to us when we hurt them. This is called humility. **The attitude of humility is essential to a healthy marriage.**

So why is it that some people refuse to say sorry, even when clearly in the wrong? Firstly, as a child they may have never been taught to take responsibility for their actions. Secondly, it may be due to false pride. A person may feel admitting they are wrong threatens their sense of self-worth. False pride may be the biggest barrier to cooperation because a person fears that apologising (or giving in) is a sign of weakness and therefore inferiority. Insecurity is typically at the root of this. If they can convince others nothing is ever their fault, they will look better and preserve their sense of dignity. However, the definition of pride can also include arrogance or conceit. A person's continual refusal to accept responsibility is often linked to these characteristics. Therefore instead of trying to look innocent, a person can come across as arrogant.

People admire those who can readily admit their own wrong and work to rectify damage done.

Have I asked for my partner's forgiveness when I have hurt them?

Do I need to ask my spouse to forgive me for a wrong attitude or behaviour?

Share with each other any hurts (these may be historical) that need to be expressed and take turns to ask forgiveness using the 4 steps identified.

~~~

If we expect perfection in our spouse, we will continually be disappointed. Sometimes it may just be the little things that cause the most irritation, like your spouse leaving the lights on in a room once they have left it. We can tell them nicely how much this frustrates us or even nag that they need to be more responsible and turn them off. Neither request will necessarily change their behaviour, so we are left with 2 choices:

1. We can continue to let the light issue cause us to feel frustrated and angry at our spouse.

2. We can accept their behaviour is not going to change, so focus on changing our own attitude. We can choose not to feed our negative emotions (or let our thoughts dwell on it) as the issue is not worth destroying a marriage over. And if we want the lights off, we make it our job to turn them off without feeling resentful.

Does my spouse have a particular behaviour that I find irritating which I can choose to accept?

"Love covers a multitude of sins"

1 Peter 4v8

Grace

While we can endeavour not to repeat hurtful behaviour, we cannot guarantee 100% that it won't happen again as sometimes the hurt we inflict is unintentional. When two people are committed to showing grace towards each other, some potential conflict can be prevented. I'll share this example:

After many interruptions I had just got myself organised to get some work done in a very limited amount of time available to me. My husband walked in the room and asked that I do a job for him. My frustration at yet another interruption caused me to say:

"I really need to do my own work now! I have a very limited amount of time. Can't it wait until later?" (It was probably the angry tone in which I said this, rather than the words I used, that had more of an impact - hey, no one's perfect!). He responded with:

"Darling this has to be done now - I have Gill waiting for this to be completed. I need it for a meeting shortly, sorry it can't be done later".

As I made a move to go with him he said,
"A little grumpy, aren't we darling? I still love you, thank you for doing this, let's have a quick hug".

He could have reacted to my grumpiness by retaliating but instead those few simple words of grace defused my anger and put a smile on my face!

Grace by definition refers to showing love, kindness and mercy that is not earned or even deserved. **A healthy relationship requires both truth and**

love. A trusting relationship will not evolve out of dishonesty. We need to own up to our failures and show an attitude of grace when we are faced with our spouse's failures.

Think of a situation where your spouse provoked your anger. Did you show love and kindness in return?

What was the outcome of how you chose to react?

In hindsight, what could you have done differently?

Strategy 7: Steps to Resolve Conflict

A marriage is either made or marred through companionship and cooperation. **If you make a commitment to consider each other's view and negotiate, you'll build a strong foundation for success.**

When conflict arises, the ultimate goal is to work towards a mutually agreed resolution. This strengthens a relationship while meeting personal needs.

I received the following description from Roger on how he and Jane try to resolve conflict:

Roger tries to talk about areas of conflict but sometimes reads too much into things. Jane shuts down and will not talk about things as she believes Roger refuses to understand or see things her way. Conversations usually end with Jane saying "Well its all me then, I'm the one with the problem. I'll have to live with it, get over it and shut up about it," which frustrates Roger immensely. He does not feel he is even looking to blame but rather wants solutions. However, solutions can only be found if problems are identified.

I wonder how Roger identifies the problems. Roger says he's not looking to blame, but it seems Jane feels the finger is pointed at her. She then retreats by saying it's her fault, which ends the discussion. Perhaps Roger needs to spend more time reflective listening so Jane feels she is understood. The conflict resolving process needs to include both Roger and Jane identifying how their behaviour contributes to the problem to end the blame game.

Our differences are not the problem; rather, it is our reaction to them that creates disharmony. The previous strategies give guidelines on effective communication and conflict resolutions skills. You will need to use these when following the six steps identified here to help you resolve conflict.

Conflict Resolution: The six steps

1. Find an appropriate time.
2. Take turns to listen to each other define the problem.
3. List the areas you both agree on and disagree on.
4. Admit how your own behaviour/attitude contributes to the problem.
5. Discuss possible solutions. Identify positively what you can both do to help and ask for the other's opinion.
6. Decide together on a course of action and be prepared to re-evaluate how successful the outcome is.

What is the best time to discuss disagreements?

When should you avoid discussing your disagreements?

Name three issues you disagree on which you would like to resolve:

Together, choose one issue and write how you each see it:

What are your spouse's thoughts and feelings on this issue? (Use their words to describe how they feel)

Continue to work through the process together to resolve the issue.

What lessons did you learn through this process that you'll continue to benefit from?

Out of conflict we can gain a deeper appreciation of how our spouse thinks and feels. Remember to ask for forgiveness where necessary and make up. While conflict causes a brief separation between couples, it can lead to a deeper intimacy when reunited.

Strategy 8: The Ultimate Say

Conflict commonly occurs through the decision making process. Developing appropriate strategies helps to reduce conflict. Often in a relationship we have strengths and expertise in different areas from our spouse. Some couples decide to leave the decision making to their spouse, in their pre-agreed upon areas of strength. For example, one partner may be particularly good at planning and budgeting, so they become responsible for deciding what should be spent in different areas. The other may be creative in decorating or landscaping, so these tasks become their responsibility.

God made males and females equal; therefore unity needs to be the objective of decision-making.   When agreement cannot be reached on a particular decision, it is best to wait before proceeding until more information is found that will help you reach agreement. If the decision needs to be made immediately, the Biblical perspective would suggest the husband makes the decision and bears the consequences of it, but only after consulting and considering the needs and best interests of his wife. He should not dictate or make the decisions independently from his wife, who maintains her own view but supports him in the decision. As I have said, the ultimate goal in decision-making is unity reached through communication. That is, both parties agree on the best course of action.

What process will the two of you use in decision-making?

Have you agreed on areas of responsibility where you can make an individual decisions?

What do you propose should happen if you cannot agree together on a course of action? Do you believe one person should have the final say?

Not all disagreements need to be completely resolved. For example, you may not agree on political issues but decide not to let it affect your relationship. Even in the strongest of marriages there is conflict. Conflict does not destroy relationships; it's the inability to resolve conflict, even if it means just letting the issue go.   Of course this is appropriate for minor matters (don't sweat the small stuff) such as buying butter or margarine. However, serious difficulties arise once couples have established a long-standing ineffective way of confronting problems. When one or both are not willing to compromise or work together on issues affecting their lifestyle, the outside help of a professional may be necessary to help break through the negative behaviour habits or patterns.

Many conflicts are the result of personality differences. We need to recognise and accept our differences, work to compliment each other, and focus on our spouse's strengths while supporting them in their weak areas. I remember reading a long time ago that the qualities which we first find the most attractive in our spouse can be the ones that drive us the most insane! My husband loved my laid back attitude when we fell in love but has since expressed his frustration at my lack of organisation around the home! Remember, each day makes a difference in our relationships; we are either growing together or apart.

For love to grow and mature it must be safeguarded by loyalty. When a relationship goes through the tough times and the "feeling" of love is not current, it will be loyalty to each other that protects the marriage from disintegrating. Loyalty to your spouse will keep you from the temptation to stray and motivate you to meet your partner's needs. Remember, your commitment to your spouse should not be based on the "feeling" of love, because feelings can change on a whim (or hormonal surge). While it is important to acknowledge how we "feel" when we're hurt or frustrated, we must do it in a way that seeks to resolve conflict peacefully.

When only one spouse is prepared to adapt, a marriage can still be improved. **Change begins with ourselves**. The advice given here will help you work towards a satisfying marriage through the changes you make and modelling the behaviour you want to see in others. By loving your spouse, you create a positive environment for them to respond to your love.

"Success is not final, failure is not fatal; it is the courage to continue that counts."

Winston Churchill

Strategy 9: Finances

A healthy attitude towards money
Money is a tool. It is a means to an end. It is the stuff we need to survive in this world. Money is one of the reasons we work. With money we buy the right to eat, live in a house, take vacations, buy clothes, pay for entertainment, and hopefully give some away to help those in greater need than ourselves.

Money is not evil, but the love of money is. If we make money our 'God' and devote our lives to the pursuit of it, we often let more important things pass us by.

Answer the following questions very honestly

Do you believe you have a healthy attitude toward money?

Does money cause problems in your family relationships?

Do you have a miserly or generous attitude to money?

What is/was your parent's attitude to money and how has this influenced you?

Are you living within your means?

Do you have debt in any shape or form which you can't repay?

What we really want to concentrate on in this section is resolving conflict where money issues are concerned in a blended family situation. If your answers above indicate problems concerning money, you will need to start there. If you recognise any money problems, these will be exacerbated in a blended family situation.

This section on money can't solve any existing budget or debt issues resulting from mismanagement. There are plenty of resources on budgeting and financial planners in your area who will be able to give you budgeting advice. Some people find it very difficult to gauge their financial situation objectively. Thus, enlisting the help of an independent professional to comprehensively assess a situation can be the best option. Many churches, particularly the larger ones, also offer this service through the help of attendees who are proficient in this area. Alternatively, contact Citizens Advice who will be able to recommend a budgeting service. I strongly suggest if you do have problems in the area of managing money seek some help quickly.

When you remarry

When a couple marry, new financial arrangements need to be made. There are a variety of arrangements possible:
- Everything is combined so all debts/assets belong to the new family unit.
- Totally separate accounts are used so both keep separate records but jointly contribute to the household expenses.
- There may be pre-nuptial agreements to contend with.
- There may be a disparity between assets, debts and income brought into the relationship.
- Ongoing financial commitments to previous partners and child support may continue.
- A combination of the above might be at work.

The main concern is developing a system and an understanding that you both feel comfortable with. You will need to consider priorities and previous spending habits. These issues need to be dealt with, discussed and planned for. Once the decisions have been made with regard to these issues they will probably need some fine tuning. In our own experience with money issues, I've found that as long as we are prepared to sit down and discuss financial commitments and future spending, there is no problem which cannot be resolved. In saying this, there does need to be give and take sometimes, particularly where attitudes to money differ. Also, we find that we can discuss an issue but not necessarily resolve it straight away. Sometimes it takes two or three attempts to come up with outcomes we are both satisfied with.

Taking time to discuss options and then reflect allows us to ponder on the other's perspective and think about things from a different angle. The important point here is the process – we've found that once we had the process established for resolving issues, as long as we stuck to the process we did get through. These processes have been covered in previous strategies.

In a blended family situation, there are certain unique aspects which need to be dealt with, because a blended family has its own unique set of circumstances. There are stepchildren, biological children, different income streams and different asset ratios. Each blended family has the potential to have a different problem financially, so we are not going to try to cover every different scenario. There is often no right or wrong approach, as long as it works for your family. So how do successful blended families deal with the issues of finance? There are two main points to keep in mind:

Firstly, it is a matter of attitude. Get your attitude right. You cannot change someone else's attitude but you can change your own. It is so important that your attitude is healthy because a healthy attitude will bring contentment. An unhealthy attitude will bring resentment and ultimately bitterness. We do not want to live our lives in our blended families bringing up our children with an attitude of resentment and bitterness. If you are openly resentful of what's spent on one particular child, expect others to pick up on this attitude also.

In my blended family there are five children between us. We encourage our children to be happy for each other. If one gets a trip or a new bike and they get something different, be happy for them and be satisfied with what you have. Now I know this is our choice and some parents would find this difficult because of the fairness issues, but overall we try to balance it out when it's within our power to. Any signs of jealousy we deal with by talking the issue through with them. Remember, while we can try to be fair when it's within our control, life is not always fair, and so we must equip our children to deal with it. The emotional security we give our children has far more value than the money we spend on them.

You'll most likely find as I have, that's it's not always possible for each child to be treated 100% equally all the time. This is not to say that one child is being disadvantaged if they miss out on something. It might be that a sibling has a talent at sports that requires more money, time and effort (transporting, uniforms, etc.) for a season than is being spent on another child. Remember to look at it from the child's point of view. They may not be bothered that Joe plays a sport and they don't. There may be some things that don't seem fair to you as a parent but are not a problem for the child. The child may only become concerned if time or money spent on another child prevents them from being able to do something.

Secondly, put what we call 'The fair and reasonable test' across all financial issues. This is self explanatory but all it actually means is to just have a second look at decisions made and assess whether your spending is both fair and reasonable. What are your motives for making the decisions you have made? If your motives are out of fear, guilt, spite, jealousy or just plain nastiness, maybe you need to rethink the decision. Bad choices don't create good consequences for you or for others.

Here are two further tips; one for men and one for women.

Men: Don't spoil your biological children by trading time spent with them, for gifts. Feelings of guilt may tempt you to do this. Children can end up deprived of important values. Even if children only have small periods of time with you, ensure its good quality time. This will have a greater long-term impact than gifts and money.

Women: If you have a husband who is paying maintenance for his children, don't give him grief about it. He has to do it! In most countries it's the law and must be done. Don't let this come between you. It's ok to vent your frustration in an appropriate manner, but don't lay the blame on him. Get your attitude right. This issue has the potential to be a relationship breaker because it won't stop until the children are grown up and supporting themselves.

Lastly, a reminder about the children caught in the middle of decision making. Remember the attitudes you practice will be passed onto to your children because they learn more by watching you than by listening to you. Get your attitudes and motives right, as they will pick up on these.

Top tips for financial health

- Plan your budget together.
- Include your financial goals; how will your budget enable you to achieve them.
- Keep detailed records of how your money is being spent, this will help you identify problem areas.
- Address family member's needs and wants.
- Discuss what arrangement is "Fair" to meet these needs and wants.
- Examine your motives on spending making sure they are right.
- Put yourself in your partner's situation, how do they think/feel about spending habits?

Part Three

~~~~~~~~~~~~~~~

Effective
Boundaries

"Correction does much, but encouragement does more."

Goethe

According to Wikipedia.org, "Discipline" means:

Any **training** *intended to produce a specific character or pattern of behaviour, especially training that produces moral, physical, or mental development in a particular direction.*

So, for the purpose of this chapter, the term "discipline" will refer to encouraging positive behaviour, not the use of physical punishment.

Discipline ideally guides children into appropriate behaviour and teaches them about actions and their consequences. If children experience this while they are still young, there is greater likelihood they will develop their own self-discipline. This equips them to make good decisions for their lives. All this sounds great in theory, but what happens when you have different parenting styles?

Unfortunately, opposite parenting styles can be the source of conflict in many blended families. It's often said that a couple in a first marriage stay together for the sake of the kids however, in a second marriage they part because of the kids! Do you fight over how to handle discipline and have opposite approaches? Well you're not alone. Many parents in a blended family face similar struggles so you'll get an opportunity to address this shortly.

We all want the best for our children - right? The truth is we cannot guarantee they will grow into well-adjusted responsible adults. However, we can do our very best to encourage them in the right direction! To achieve this we must firstly be a parent to our children. Along with providing the necessities of life (e.g. food, shelter, love), parenting includes guiding children in a way that helps them reach their fullest potential. Through positive parenting (discipline) we train and encourage our children to become responsible adults of integrity. Now let's get on with it!

"Wise discipline imparts wisdom; spoiled adolescents embarrass their parents."

Proverbs 29:15

Strategy 1: Parenting Styles

Our parenting style is greatly influenced by what we have experienced during our childhood. We may have had a parent who operated one way and we're determined to do it differently with our own children. For example, if you had a parent who continually yelled, you may strive not to yell at your children. However, it's not uncommon to hear our parent's voices coming out of our mouths! Here's Gavin's experience:

"Good communication is a must. I've learned that people can parent much differently depending on how they were raised as kids."

Gavin

Even in a stable first marriage with both biological parents, there are challenges. In a blended family, other influences complicate matters such as an ex-partner's or stepparent's conflicting expectations.

When we become parents, be it planned or unplanned, we need to step up to the awesome responsibility of nurturing and training our children. Parents may have different styles but we can still commit to doing the best job possible within our power. We can't parent for someone else; it's something we have to do on our own for our child. This is our responsibility.

It's important to complete the next exercise based on **your own** experience of parenting.

Which parenting style do you identify with?

The Controller

This person wants to be in complete **control.** They call the shots. Their way is the only way and all others must conform to it. They don't feel the need to communicate or discuss their approach because they believe they are always right. Yes, the Controller may get children to obey them but they have a harsh approach to discipline and tend to invoke fear, not respect.

The Planner

He/she is considerate of others views and has **plans** in place to encourage positive behaviour. They have a clear idea of their goals as a parent and aren't afraid to ask for help if necessary. The Planner takes note of individual needs and adjusts the plan accordingly. They celebrate success and consistently enforce consequences in line with their behaviour plan.

The Pleaser

The Pleaser will **retreat** from confrontation, particularly if they have a Controller partner. They want to keep the peace to ensure everyone is happy. They keep quiet to avoid conflict but feel frustrated when a system isn't working. They can develop a good plan but are prone to inconsistency in following it through. They want to rescue children from consequences.

Note:

This person may have been a planner in a previous relationship but now guilt motivates their behaviour. They fear their children will reject them if they enforce consequences for misbehaviour. They believe the best thing they can do to make up for their mistakes (divorce/separation) is keep everyone happy. They may **ignore problems** and buy their children gifts to alleviate their own guilt.

The Absent Parent

This parent is absorbed in their own world and may feel put out when others want to interrupt them. Sadly they miss out on taking an active role in family life. Their priorities are elsewhere. They may spoil their children with material gifts to ease their conscience but fail to give them their time. They can be physically present but emotionally unavailable to their children.

How did your mother/father (or significant other) parent?

Mother figure

Father figure

Now consider your own parenting style:

What style/s of parenting do you identify with?

What reasons influence your choice to parent this way?

The great thing about parenting is we can change our style. Don't beat yourself up if you aren't happy with your style – choose to change!

Opposite Parenting Styles?
If you and your partner have opposite parenting styles don't try and counterbalance your partner. For example, if you think they are too harsh on a child, don't try to over-compensate for their parenting by being too soft. It is your job to role model a **balanced parenting style**, not to counteract some else's style.

I'll share with you Penny's experience of having an opposite parenting style to her partner's.

"Joe tries to discipline my children; he's constantly on their case and on mine about them. He continually puts them down, along with my parenting abilities. Consequently we are always fighting because I want him to lay off the kids. I should discipline but he won't let me...it's not good enough. He constantly ignores what I say and goes and does it himself or behind my back."

Penny

Did you pick up that Joe is a Controller? A scenario like this is not about the children and their behaviour but the relationship between the adults.

Success Strategy:
Trying to understand and appreciate why someone uses a particular parenting style is the first step in working towards common goals. Discuss (don't judge) together the beliefs and experiences that have shaped the way each of you parent. This includes looking at how you were parented as a

child; what was good and what do you hope to do differently as a result of your experience.

Share with your partner:

- ✓ What you hope to achieve as a parent
- ✓ How you intend to achieve this
- ✓ Changes you need to make
- ✓ How you can support each other

Parents must discuss the issue of discipline and go through the conflict resolving process (Part 2) to reach agreement on boundaries and consequences. In Penny's family, this unresolved conflict harms their relationship and creates a tense environment for everyone. The point I want to emphasise here is that the children's behaviour does not destroy the relationship although they often become the target for blame. The key issue is a couple's inability to work together to find solutions they are both comfortable with.

I'll now share some guidelines for you to use as a foundation for positive parenting. **These guidelines will help you form a strategy for discipline so your blended family can succeed!**

"We try to work together on discipline. I think Gary is too strict, and he thinks I am too easy. I have helped him to lighten up a little and he has helped me to be more firm and consistent. We both agree on that. I still wish he would lighten up and he wishes I would be stricter."

Pam

Pam and Gary are on the right road here because they are working together to minimise future conflict – now I'll help them and you along the journey.

Strategy 2: Setting Boundaries

Rules, laws, regulations and expectations govern every area of our life outside our family home. Our employer expects us to complete our tasks; the law requires us to pay for our goods; our personal safety requires that we drive within the speed limit. These boundaries serve to protect us, keep us honest and encourage us to behave fairly.

Sports are a great example of why parameters are necessary. Let's imagine we are on our way to a game. What do the players need to make sure they play to the best of their ability?

- **Coach**: This needs to be someone who explains the rules of the game, lets the players know what the expectations are and how to score for their side.

- **Training schedule**: This makes sure the players are properly equipped for the positions they are to play in.

- **Knowledge of the rules and penalties**: There shouldn't be any surprises as far as penalties go. The players should know they will be penalised if they are offside, break the rules, or don't show up at practices.

When players know the rules, they can get in and have fun with the game. Imagine the chaos that would occur if a sports game was played without the guidance of a coach and rules! Think of the qualities a great manager/ teacher/ or coach that makes them so good. Your list might include: great communicator; fair; firm; has high standards; not afraid to help out with a difficult task; fun and rewarding.

View yourself as a coach in your family and bring the rest of the team on board!

Top sports people must train regularly and they are not afraid of discipline.

Your team can include reserves such as friends, grandparents, teachers or pastors who can come on board to support you to play well.

Now focus on your blended family. Think about what boundaries or expectations of behaviour you feel are appropriate for children in the following areas.

Chores	Meal times
Behaviour when entertaining	Behaviour when out
Bedtimes	Alcohol, cigarettes, and drugs
Sharing of possessions	Personal hygiene
Allowances	Friends over
Food	Sibling rivalry
Language, voice tone, manners	Conversation, social skills
Care of own possessions	Respect for other's possessions
Attitudes	Resolving conflict
Personal safety	Music listened to
Use of TV, play stations, computers, phones	

Some of these areas may not cause any problems but you may think of others that do.

With your spouse, make a list of the five most important areas (theses might be current problem areas) you want to positively direct the step/bio children's behaviour in. Write the expected behaviour you want to encourage in each area. For example: Language; family members are to speak respectfully to each other using appropriate manners. Chores; these are to be completed within the given time frame, without fuss.

Expectation:
1.
2.
3.
4.
5.

These expectations become the guidelines for the way your family operates. Every expectation can be encouraged or discouraged through the use of consequences. We'll come back to this soon.

Discipline is the area some couples find the hardest to handle.

"It is hard work. Our relationship is great when my partner's children aren't around but when they are, our relationship suffers."

Have you negotiated a plan together for encouraging positive behaviour based on the expectations you identified? Many couples in a blended family have difficulty doing this. If you want your family to succeed, take time to complete the exercises included here.

We all want to raise our children in a fun and positive environment. If we have too many rules and regulations, we risk children rebelling so it's important to find a balance. Don't "sweat the small stuff". Try to say "Yes" as much as possible in areas that are not detrimental to their character for example, hair colour. Use your common sense to guide you. As children grow older, along with increasing responsibilities should come increased but appropriate freedom.

To help guide children in decision-making, give them choices. Children need to be encouraged to make decisions from a young age. They learn about consequences through the decision making process. For a small child, it might be what they want on their toast. Give them control over things that are not so important so when you do say "No", it has meaning and impact. If they continually hear "No" they will become resentful or immune to it's meaning. When a child asks why the answer is "No", do you ever recall hearing a parent saying "Because I said so"? If you want your children's respect you must be firm but fair. **Always be prepared to support your answers to their question with good reasons. This shows a child you have their best interests at heart** - you're not saying no to be mean or make their life difficult.

Do you have in place a planned approach to discipline?

Are your children/step children aware of your expectations and the associated consequences?

Are you consistent with the consequences?

The five expectations you have identified form the guidelines for encouraging desirable behaviour in your blended family. These expectations need consequences linked to them. The consequences must be communicated to every person.

Rules with secure boundaries (consequences) give children a sense of security.

Who's in control in your home?

As parents we can use discipline to teach children to behave in the right manner with the right attitude. Expectations and consequences help children learn about consequences for their actions.

Consequences teach a child about good behaviour they're rewarded for, or negative behaviour which has an unpleasant outcome.

What happens when we don't discipline or set boundaries which are reinforced with consequences? Children who are not disciplined may lack self-discipline, feel insecure, be disobedient, lack respect for others and direction.

It can be hard as a loving parent to discipline our children but it shows we are concerned about their character development. **Children need a clear understanding of right and wrong to give direction to their lives.** As a parent, our greatest responsibility is to nurture and guide our children. The training methods we use influence how our children should live.

Guilt: The psychological barrier to discipline

"My husband will not discipline in case his children say they would rather stay with their mother"

Alice

Unfortunately this is so common. It can be difficult for non-custodial parents to enforce consequences for their children's undesirable behaviour, for fear they won't enjoy their time or decide they no longer want to visit. A parent can choose to ignore bad behaviour to keep the peace with their child. Stepparents as a result, often believe their stepchildren are spoiled. Many stepparents have told me when they challenge the bio parent about this, they (the bio parent) become defensive and the stepparent becomes the one with the problem! If this is the case in your blended family, read on and I will guide you both in finding the right approach.

"My husband believes his children have been through a nightmare with his divorce from his first wife so he needs to continually make up for that and I just have to put up with it. I am dissatisfied with our relationship. His children can do no wrong when it comes to someone else like me having a say."

Blended families have evolved out of pain (the death or separation of a parent). Many parents feel bad about the turmoil this pain has caused their children. They often carry guilt or blame themselves for having failed their children and want to protect their children from more distress or upset. If a child misbehaves, a bio parent many not enforce consequences because they want to avoid causing their child further pain. Basically, they just want their child to be happy. This may sound familiar: "They've been through enough already without us (parent/stepparent) getting down on them".

Firstly we must accept, "There is no such thing as a perfect parent". We will fail our children at times regardless of whether we are divorced or not. There's plenty we can feel guilty about if we want to. Do each of your children eat 5 servings of fruit and vegetables a day? Do they watch less than one hour of TV a week? Do you sometimes pretend you're listening to them when you didn't understand a word they said?

Secondly, there are some things we have no control over, like the death of a spouse or our partner deserting us. There is no need to accept responsibility or carry the guilt for these things. What we can do is accept responsibility for those specific things we do have control over, such as our contribution to a marriage breakdown or the failure to meet children's needs in other ways, such as neglect, disciplining out of anger, or lack of support and encouragement. Since we can't approach problems with the benefit of hindsight, we have to learn our way through them which will entail making some mistakes. Further down the track we can look back and may be able to identify how we could have done things differently. Be assured that all of us experience failures and carry feelings of guilt, but we must forgive ourselves.

"I said to myself, "I will confess my wrong doing to the Lord." And you forgave me! All my guilt is gone."

Psalm 32v5

We can't change past events. We can take responsibility for our actions that have caused others pain, by acknowledging our wrong and apologising where appropriate. However, we need to let go of the past and the guilt associated with it and plan for the future.

It is appropriate to apologise to our children for hurt our actions have caused them. It's normal for them to grieve the loss of their biological parents' relationship but, we need to encourage them to accept the reality of the situation and move forward. **Constantly trying to please children by not disciplining them or buying material gifts to ease our conscience or guilt will not free them from the pain or turmoil they have gone through.** In fact, these actions may serve as a continual reminder to the child by encouraging a "Poor me" mentality. Don't focus on making up for the past; instead work towards a healthy future.

Now remember the example of the sports team. Imagine the players being on the field that wasn't marked with lines. They have some idea of how far they can go but until they have gone beyond the boundary they don't think the penalty is for real. It's vital that you let children know what the rules are. Don't be afraid of training them and letting them know you are their coach. Boundaries give security and freedom. **Don't make excuses for your children's behaviour out of guilt; dealing appropriately (and lovingly) with undesirable behaviour develops your child's character.** Consistent boundaries and responsibilities will provide a secure environment and strong foundation for a child's future.

It's a common misbelief that children won't love you if you discipline them. Children are looking to you as a parent, not as a friend. They can find friends anywhere, but they can't find a mum or dad anywhere. If you only see your children for shorts bursts of time, remember that they still need you to be their parent. We all desire to be connected with something that gives us identity and purpose. It could be work, a sports team, a school or a church. Whatever it is, nothing can replace family and the significant part of our identity that comes from our parents. Children will love and respect a parent who is fair and consistent with encouraging rules. Remember the moment we set foot outside our home, we are governed by rules. What better place than in the home to learn how to respond to those rules!

When your children come to visit they want to belong; they don't just want to be guests. To help them feel they belong, give them some age appropriate responsibilities and age appropriate consequences if they break the rules. Don't spoil your children with excessive material gifts or outings to show your love, which can be tempting for those parents who don't have regular access. You cannot buy your child's love and respect. What they want and need is quality time with you and the protection of boundaries.

Accept responsibility for your actions and their consequences, but focus on the future. Allowing guilt to motivate your parenting is destructive to the marriage relationship. For children to respect their parents, there must be a structure of boundaries and consequences. If children know they can take advantage of others, get away with defiant behaviour and/or are given things on a whim, they feel insecure for lack of boundaries. Make a positive plan that focuses on how you can be the best parent (you'll never be perfect) from now on!

Do you find it hard to discipline your children? Why?

Have you forgiven yourself for the mistakes you have made as a parent? Write down how you plan on moving forward.

How will boundaries and consequences help your child/children?

Strategy 3: How to Discipline

There are two parts to discipline:

1. The expectation; identifying the behaviour you want to encourage
2. Consequences to encourage this behaviour

We have looked at expectations in Strategy 2 (boundaries), which are important in your family. We will now focus on how to communicate and encourage adherence to these.

1. Communicate the expectations
This might be during a family meeting with all members. Make sure everyone is familiar with the expected behaviour you want to encourage, and the consequences of non-compliance. Avoid finger pointing or laying blame when discussing expectations. Say for example, one child is particularly disrespectful. Don't single them out by saying "You must...". Instead use the guideline, "In our family we will speak respectfully to each other".

2. Request the behaviour you want
This refers to the first time you ask the child to comply with the request.

3. State the expectation and consequence
Remind them of the rule and consequences of non-compliance.

4. Use encouragement or consequences
Reinforce the positive behaviour or discourage undesirable behaviour with appropriate action.

5. Reconcile
Discuss the lesson learned. Identify:

    - What caused the problem?
    - How do they feel?
    - What behaviour was expected?
    - **Reassure them of your love/support**

For example:
1. The expectation is that everyone is responsible for looking after their own possessions and keeping them tidy.
Katherine notices that Jenny has dumped her jacket in the middle of the kitchen floor.

2. Katherine makes a request:
"Jenny, would you mind picking up you jacket and putting it away?"
Jenny ignores Katherine.

3. Katherine reminds Jenny of the expectation:
"Jenny, you know your father and I have agreed that each of us must take care of our own belongings; please put your jacket away now or you will not be allowed to watch TV tonight (knows her favourite program is on)".

4. If Jenny complies, Katherine says,
"Thank heaps Jenny, I appreciate it. The place looks so much tidier when we all do our bit."
If Jenny doesn't comply, Katherine says,
"I see you've chosen to not watch TV tonight. It's a shame you'll miss out on your favourite program."

5. Katherine will need to make an appropriate time to follow this up along the lines of:
"Jenny, do you remember why you're not able to watch TV now - how do you feel about that?"
"What would have been a better choice of action?"
"I feel frustrated at the mess when clothes are left on the floor. We want to encourage everyone to be responsible and really appreciate it when you are. You're a very special part of our family and we value your contribution. Let's make sure you don't have to miss out on that TV program again."

It's important for the child's self esteem to separate the behaviour from the child. **Love the child, but dislike the undesirable behaviour**. Never label a child as naughty, otherwise that's how they will think about themselves. The child's **behaviour** may be 'naughty', but not the child.

One more point; to be effective, the **consequences must have significance**. There's no point in making a child do the vacuuming if they love it, or taking away their bike for the week if they don't like riding it!

When you make a request:

- Ensure you have the child's attention
- Use eye contact
- If the child is young, get down to their level

It's hopeless shouting a request across the room if the child is totally absorbed in an activity. They are unlikely to take notice of you.

Discipline must be fair to be effective. If a child is in the middle of doing something, give them a time frame in which you would like your request done. Remind them if necessary but don't fall into the trap of nagging. Follow up with consequences if it is not done when agreed. You as the adult are in charge and therefore have the final say, but allow them to express their opinion. It is wise to be flexible and negotiate, particularly with older children. It is unreasonable to say "Jump" and expect the child to do it immediately despite the full glass of juice in their hand. If they ask to either put it down or drink it first, (a bit tongue-in-cheek but I trust you get the point) let them! Children are not robots; treat them with the same respect you want to be treated with. If you yell at them, expect them to yell at their siblings and you as well! After all, **children will learn more from watching your behaviour than from listening to you**.

Are you familiar with the golden rule? Here's the original version:

"Do for others what you would like them to do for you."
                                                                        Matthew 7v12

To avoid the use of punishment, it is vital to reinforce positive behaviour. Benefits of complying can be reinforced with a reward system. This might be appropriate for keeping one's room tidy, using manners, helping out when not asked by doing dishes etc. The following is an example of the system one family uses to encourage appropriate behaviour.

"We sit with all the children in a family meeting which we have once a month and come up with acceptable behaviours, privileges as well as consequences. Everything is then printed out and placed on the bulletin board. All the kids as well as my husband and I know what we have to do. The kids know before hand what will happen according to what behaviour they choose to do, so we do not have just one parent being the disciplinarian, but if a major crisis happens, the biological parent of that child will take over the discipline. Thankfully that doesn't happen often. We have a points system, and you have to earn a certain amount of points before any privilege is earned for that week."

Strategy 4: Consequences

The topic of discipline is usually associated with 'punishment'. **Punishment is a negative consequence** for an undesirable behaviour. However, **positive reinforcement is a crucial part of discipline** that is sometimes overlooked.

Positive reinforcement focuses on and rewards good behaviour.

To enable a child to associate a reward with the behaviour, reinforcement should be immediate. The following are examples of positive reinforcement:

- Words of encouragement
- Body language, a smile, affection
- Privileges
- Outings, activities
- Material items

A parent's positive attention is a very powerful form of reinforcement. For some children, a star chart can work well too. A list is made up of 'good behaviour' and each time the child behaves positively, they receive a star. Stars can be removed for inappropriate behaviour. Once the child has reached a set number such as 30, they are taken on a special outing or can stay up to watch a movie. This is only limited by your creativity. The lesson here is that with privileges, come responsibilities. **Responsible behaviour can be reinforced with privileges.**

Extinction is another form of discipline I will mention here. This form includes:

1. Ignoring bad behaviour:

Do not respond until the child behaves correctly.

2. Removing privileges or items of esteem:

Take away things your child enjoys.

3. Time out:

Place them in a safe area without toys, TV, etc. until they have calmed down. A minute per year of their age is a good guide; this is great for young children and tantrums.

The purpose of extinction is to remove indirect positive reinforcement for bad behaviour. For example, if a child whines you have three choices:

- Refuse to listen until the child makes a request in a respectful manner, "When you ask nicely I will listen"
- Remove an item they enjoy using
- Place them in a room by themselves until they stop

All forms of consequences need to be prompt, consistent and fair to be effective.

When choosing a form of discipline, make sure it is age appropriate and in line with the action. Try to choose natural consequences; if a child deliberately throws a glass and breaks it, they could clean up the mess and contribute towards a new one.

Here are two more forms of discipline or ways of encourage desirable behaviour:

Redirecting:
Direct the child's attention to positive behaviour. This is a favourite one of mine that I use regularly with my youngest strong-willed son. One of the best ways of redirecting is through the use of choices. When you command a child to "Come and sit here" they can comply or not. If you say, "What chair would you like to come and sit in, the blue one or the green one?", they are now thinking about the chairs, not whether they will comply.

Redirecting can be very useful when a child wants to do something a parent feels is inappropriate. If the parent directs the child's attention to something else, the focus is taken off the undesirable behaviour. Try saying, "How about we go and …..".

Grounding:
Restricting your child to stay in one place, usually home. This is appropriate for older children and might be used if they've broken a curfew. It prevents them from going out as they had planned as a consequence of their disobedience.

Here are some suggestions for age appropriate consequences. When using the techniques below remember to state the instruction and remind the child of the rule as outlined in Strategy 3.

Birth - 2 years
- Positive reinforcement
- Redirecting

3 - 12 years
- Positive reinforcement
- Redirecting
- Time out to age 6 or 7 years
- Withdrawing privileges
- Grounding

13 - 18 years
- Positive reinforcement
- Withdrawing privileges
- Grounding

You may have noticed that I haven't mentioned smacking. It's effectiveness as a deterrent to bad behaviour is controversial. In New Zealand it is now illegal so I strongly advise against it.

Children are more likely to misbehave if they are tired, hungry, bored, neglected or feeling unwell. **Keep in tune with where they're at emotionally and physically, as this will help you decide appropriate consequences.** Explore the motive for their behaviour; is it to directly defy you or is their behaviour a reflection of where they're at in general? If they are grumpy because they're tired, an early night may be the best consequence!

Knowing and appreciating each child's personality can help you here. I remember getting frustrated with one of my stepchildren's refusal to do a task when asked. I began to take it personally thinking they were just using the chance to defy me. As it happens, this behaviour was typical in many situations due to their choleric personality. I eventually found that if I made a request, I had far more success. I started asking "When do you think you could do this?" as opposed to "Please do this now" and then used a reminder if necessary "You said you would …has this changed?". This gave them a feeling of control and a greater willingness to comply.

Finally, **don't let children manipulate you into letting them escape consequences**. They may try-it-on with phrases such as, "It's your entire fault" or "If you hadn't done that, I wouldn't have…". Every action has a consequence. Allow them to experience the consequences of their undesirable actions so they will avoid repeating them.

✓ Discuss with your spouse the discipline process and consequences in Strategies 3 and 4.

✓ Choose a system you think will work for your family that identifies ways of encouraging positive behaviour and responding to undesirable behaviour. For example, hold a family meeting and ask children for their input on expectations, or to help brainstorm consequences. Your system might include putting a list of guidelines on the fridge where they can be referred to regularly.

✓ Look again at the expectations you identified in Strategy 2. Link consequences to your five expectations.

Write your system here:

Read through the following strategies carefully; they are crucial to your success.

Success Strategies

• Parents are children's advocates: never compromise their safety.

• Keep children safe and secure with reasonable rules and natural consequences.

• Communicate clearly expectations and consequences.

• Don't sweat the small stuff.

• Avoid reacting emotionally; give yourself timeout if necessary before implementing consequences.

• Keep well and look after yourself so you **don't punish out of anger and tiredness;** it's easy to do when we're under pressure.

• Celebrate success!!

- All children like to be noticed; bad attention is better than no attention so give plenty of praise for good behaviour. Often when a child receives positive attention the problem behaviour will go away.

- Focus on the goal; the ultimate reward is your child growing into a self-disciplined adult.

- Don't give up; if the cycle needs to be broken, you can do it!

- Children are clever; they watch you and know what your weaknesses are. Be firm and kind, consistent and fair.

- Present a united front (more on this shortly).

- Use the effective communication techniques outlined in Part 2 with children.

- Encourage children to take responsibility for their actions.

- Children **will** test the boundaries to see what happens; be prepared!

It only takes one generation to change dysfunction in a family!

When you are on the right track to being a firm and loving parent, your conversations will sound like these:

- *"You're late again mate, we need to work this out together."*

- *"I wish I could let you stay up longer, but we agreed on this time. Besides, remember how tired you get when you miss your sleep."*

- *"When we both cool off, let's talk about what needs to be done."*

- *"You say all your friends will be there. Could you get me some more information?"*

The effects on your children if you are firm and loving:

- A healthy self respect

- Self control

- Security

- Open communication with parents: it reduces tension, adds stability and helps prevent rebellion
- A willingness to obey rules and authority

Take time to evaluate your system's effectiveness and make any necessary changes.

Evaluating Your System

To help evaluate how effective your plan is, ask yourselves whether the following statements reflect your experience:

1. We present a united front to the children.
2. I respectfully make requests taking each child's age and understanding into consideration.
3. The children know, depending on their actions, what the consequences will be.
4. The consequences have significance and work to encourage/ discourage behaviour.
5. The children are rewarded or encouraged for positive behaviour.
6. I am fair and reasonable in my approach.
7. I don't discipline out of anger.
8. My duty as a parent to train and discipline is done without guilt.
9. My children respect me as an authority figure.

Strategy 5: Presenting a United front

When parents fail to agree on or communicate about issues concerning children, the children are given power to make parents work against each other. For example, Ben may go and ask one parent if he can go out after the other parent has already said "No", in the hope that the second time and with a different parent, he gets a "Yes". Children can be motivated to play parents off for any of the following reasons:

1. To gain materially from a situation
2. To gain freedom from restrictions or rules
3. To avoid consequences of their actions
4. To get their own way
5. As manipulation to gain attention

The common theme here is the intended outcome works to the child's advantage. It would be pointless for a child to play parents off if, in the long run it disadvantaged them. While it works to the child's advantage, it causes conflict with a marriage if parents (step and biological) have not agreed on their approach. **We need to ensure this destructive behaviour is actively discouraged or not reinforced by the child getting his/her own way.** We will look at presenting a united front both within the home (stepparent and biological parent) and between the homes where the biological parents have parted.

Within Your Home
You and your spouse may have different expectations for an area of behaviour. For example, Reuben might think it entirely appropriate for children to help themselves to food in the house any time they want. June, on the other hand, gets very frustrated when she comes to use something in dinner preparation only to find it eaten or whole packets of treat food consumed by one person. June has 3 options.

1. She could talk to the children and tell them her expectations however, she is in trouble if her stepchildren go against her wishes because they can turn to their father for support and thus divide the couple.
2. She can discuss the matter with Ruben and come to an arrangement that they both feel comfortable with using the process in Part 2.
3. She could put food she wants to use in meal preparation in another place that is not a free-for-all area so it's there when needed.

This last option is possibly the best as it avoids the need for consequences, which must be readily enforced if you go to the trouble of outlining expectations (remember, don't sweat the small stuff). Those who have spent time around children will tell you that everyone reacts differently to rules or expectations according to their personality type. Some children by nature are readily compliant and eager to please. Others will test the boundaries time and time again.

In the above example, June could tell two children her expectation that unopened food in the pantry is not to be touched and to be fair with what they eat. For example, if there are 4 cakes, eat one and leave the rest for other family members. One child would happily oblige while the other may take no notice or "forget" the conversation. The forgetful child may need consequences to help them remember the expectation, such as no dessert one night while the others are having some. It is the consequences that will have the biggest influence on changing this child's behaviour, not repetitive requests. Obviously, to be successful, both the step and biological parent must support the behaviour request and the consequences otherwise the child only needs to play the parents/step parents against each to avoid an unpleasant outcome. And, if they are successful in avoiding the consequences, they might as well continue the behaviour. After all, why leave 3 cakes, when you can get away with eating all four!

Preventing the opportunity for children to play parents off is the best way of dealing with this issue.

"How do I get my husband to back me, or how do we present a united front to his son when it comes to chores or household rules? I don't believe my husband should side with his son over me when it comes to household chores. The only thing I ask is that his son picks up his clothes off the bedroom floor, throw out his empty pop cans, and hang up his wet towels. I really do not think those are unreasonable expectations for a 17 year old. I feel frustrated, and isolated. It is very tough being the stepparent when the biological parent's bond with his son overrides anything I have to say. I feel insignificant."

Beth

Beth currently feels unappreciated and dissatisfied. She and her husband need to make each other's needs their top priority and unite together to tackle the issue of chores. They must reach agreement on expectations and consequences. She is not being unreasonable with her requests. To overcome these issues, Beth and her husband can put into practice the material covered in Part 2 to help them reach agreement on a plan. The strategies outlined in this part can form a basis for their plan.

Have you and your spouse discussed the five most important expectations and consequences in your home? If you are successful in achieving unity with this, it reduces a child's ability to play you against each other.

Boundaries achieve their purpose when both parents agree on them and are prepared to enforce the consequences otherwise they become pointless.

Success Strategies

- If you suspect you are being played against the other parent, avoid making a decision until you have checked with them regarding their view.

- Devise an appropriate consequence for playing adults off that actively discourages this behaviour.

- Take the power away from the child by discussing your expectations in advance with all adults concerned so you are clear where everyone stands.

- Resolve the issue privately together where there is discrepancy of opinion; present a united outcome together to the child.

- **The stability of your marriage relationship forms the foundation for success; show you support your spouse, and present a united front.**

One thing that destroys many relationships

Never side with your child over your spouse in front of them. It encourages them to disrespect your spouse. **Don't do it.** Plan in advance what you will do when an issue crops up that you and your spouse disagree on. Make a commitment that you will talk it out privately before addressing the behaviour with the child.

Aim to have these discussions outside of a disagreement over parenting. Talk when you both are calm. Avoid fighting in front of children, especially over parenting issues; the child will feel they are to blame for the conflict when the problem is the adult's lack of unity. Turn the problems into opportunities for growth as you explore new solutions together.

"I guess if I could start over in my relationship I would do a couple things differently. Firstly I would make sure Ben and I are a team and support each other's decisions about parenting. I would let him be more involved with the parenting of my son. Secondly, I would make sure my son understood that Ben and I were a team who supported each other."

Alana

How **will** you and your partner support each other to enforce expectations?

Strategy 6: Parental Responsibilities

"Every area of our relationship is more than satisfactory except for discipline. We hold different beliefs and perspectives about what a stepparent's role is in correction and discipline. 'If' the stepparent is allowed to discipline, to what degree or when should they do so?"

Brent

Guidelines:
- Together decide on the rules, chores and consequences you are both comfortable with.
- Together be responsible for encouraging adherence to the rules, be united and support each other.
- Both reinforce positive behaviour.

- **Let the biological parent wherever possible enforce the punishment or consequences for defying the rules.**

While some stepparents may struggle to accept this last point, it serves to protect them. A child's loyalties will lie with their biological parent as this bond tends to be stronger than the stepparent/child bond (more on this in Part 4). Unless a stepparent has the biological parents' **full support**, they run risk of the step child not obeying because they're not their mum or dad. A child can feel this gives them the right to question a stepparent's authority. This is especially true in the early stages of a relationship. Trust and respect must be developed before a stepparent takes a more active role.

Mathew told me how discipline works in his blended family.

"At present their mother is responsible for discipline. However this changes when she becomes frustrated or fed up with the children's behaviour and then asks me to 'deal' with them. This is a role I believe is unfair to me and confusing to the children. It makes me the 'bad guy'."

In this scenario mum is sabotaging the children's relationship with their stepfather by wanting him to handle the bad behaviour, as any resentment will then be directed at him. She also risks losing her children's respect by not enforcing the consequences herself. Mathew could direct his energies at encouraging the children to respect the house rules and supporting his wife to implement any negative consequences.

"My stepdaughter is prone to temper tantrums and whining which I feel needs to be addressed. Her Dad just gives into this, which causes a lot of turmoil in me. I am allowed to cook for her, wash her clothes, bathe her, help her with her homework and baby sit her when her dad is busy with work or hobbies. However, I have no "authority" to discipline her as I would my own children who live in the same house, and from whom I would never tolerate such dramatic outbursts. Occasionally when we speak of such matters, he tells me that I will never love his children as I do my own, and I will never treat them as good as I treat my own so I bend over backwards to do things for them (I don't find it too hard because I do love them), but I never see him going out of his way for my children and seldom for his own. Why am I expected to be everything to everybody?"

Lisa

Lisa does not need to feel totally powerless in the area of discipline. She and her husband can share the responsibility for devising and monitoring boundaries and encouraging positive behaviour. She can certainly encourage her stepdaughter to adhere to the agreed upon expectations. All the children in the house need to know what is expected of them and the consequences for misbehaviour; there shouldn't be any surprises. This brings us to the issue of fairness.

Fairness

- The rules should be the same for all children at similar ages or levels of understanding.

- Do not let siblings discipline each other; they can encourage one another in positive behaviour but must remember they are a brother or sister, not a parent.

- Ensure the rules are enforced for all; don't let some get away with behaviour that others are punished for.

Be aware that children in a shared custody arrangement will go through a "settling back in period" after being with their other parent. Each child can react differently: some may be generally quiet or subdued and others may be overactive and attention seeking. Allow them time to adjust - usually 24 hours. You may also find a child withdraws emotionally before making the transition back to the other parent's house. This can be their way of coping with the process of having to say good-bye.

Strategies for Stepparents:

- Support the biological parent to enforce consequences whenever possible.
- Don't enforce consequences unless there are pre-agreed rules and consequences the children are familiar with.
- Use phrases such as "You know that your father/mother and I do not like this behaviour" and "In our family we have agreed to…" to give strength to your request.

- ◆ Reinforce positive behaviours.

- ◆ Don't dwell on negative behaviour; encourage the biological parent to address this.

- ◆ Keep the biological parent involved by asking their opinion on what to do or how to handle a situation when new ones arise.

Strategies for Biological Parents:

- ◆ Empower stepparents by devising a behaviour plan together.

- ◆ Support them in reminding your children to abide by the rules, e.g. "Your stepmother has already told you what we expect; if you don't listen we will have to…."

- ◆ You are on the same team; work with your partner to help your children become healthy, responsible adults.

- ◆ Keep the stepparent informed of activities or decisions your child makes or matters of concern that your child has discussed with you.

Different Homes, Different Rules

You cannot control what happens in another person's home. Children can and will adapt to different rules in different environments. Grandma will have one set of rules, school with have another, sports or social groups and church will again have different expectations. Don't let the fact that there are different rules in each home be an excuse not to enforce the rules in yours.

Focus on what you can control, not what you can't. If you are consistent in your approach and children are familiar with your expectations, it becomes much easier for them to adapt to the rules. An ex-partner may try to control what happens in your home; for example, they tell children not to listen the stepparent. You may not be able to prevent this. What you can do is encourage the expectation that a child will listen and respect the stepparent through the use of consequences. In such cases it may be beneficial to discuss the issue with the child. Don't place them in a position where they are taking sides or feel the need to defend the absent bio parent. Gently explain the rules in your house and the benefits of respecting them.

Refuse to be drawn into battle with the ex-partner. Don't place the child in the middle to carry messages between the adults. It's detrimental to their emotional wellbeing and fuels resentment amongst everyone. Stick to the plan you've developed.

Children only have the power to play parents off in areas the parents disagree on. This is something all children do at some stage and can range from minor matters, such as asking one for a candy after the other has said no, to complaining that one parent is not fair because they won't allow them to have boy/girlfriends for the night, while the other will. The dynamics here can be trickier for obvious reasons. As the biological parents no longer live together there is less opportunity for them to communicate and agree on issues. Despite this, ideally you are both on the same side, wanting the best for your children.

To achieve the best possible outcome for children, biological parents should work together towards solutions. This means discussing any issues of concern including discipline matters. This can be difficult when there has been a breakdown in your relationship, but children benefit when their parents can put aside their own agendas and work towards their children's best interests. I know when parents have met to do just this, it's often surprised them to learn that behaviour they discouraged but were led to believe was acceptable in the other household, was in fact, not. As children become older, they can be included in these meetings so all are fully aware of the expectations and the consequences in both households.

Can you arrange to meet with the ex-partner to discuss important matters concerning your children?

What issues do you feel would be most beneficial for both biological parents to present a united front on?

Remember, the goal is to work together towards your children's best interests; it is beneficial both in the short and long term for everyone to work with each other, not against each other. It's also much easier to prepare in advance what your approach will be to a situation. If possible, as well as discussing specific issues with your ex-partner, address the following questions:

1. What will you do if a child has been disciplined in your home, then rings their other parent to complain they're being unfairly treated?

2. What will you do if your child/stepchild is taking about what goes on at their other home in terms of discipline and complains about their treatment?

In both cases it's important that the adult talking with the child does **not pass judgment on what happens in the other home - after all you have only heard one side**. Instead reinforce to the child that rules in both homes must be respected. You also have the option of raising the issue privately with the ex-partner to ask for their side if you are concerned. Again, in the above cases, you are only hearing one side of the story from the child. If they are playing their parents against each other, you can guarantee the story they tell you will be to their advantage.

Take a moment to reflect on Colleen's experience:

"I would like to help my step daughter feel safe and secure and loved in our home. I would also like to help her to overcome lying and stop being manipulative. My stepdaughter fights with her mom almost every weekend; she is rude and disrespectful to her and does whatever she wants when she's at her mom's house. Many weekends she will call me crying on the phone to come pick her up, as she had been fighting with her mom and wanted to come home."

Colleen

In response to Colleen's request for help, we know that children need boundaries and reassurance to feel loved and secure. Colleen also told me she has a very difficult relationship with the ex-wife (mother). If the stepdaughter is arguing with her mother, chances are it's because the mother is unhappy with her behaviour. If the stepparent "rescues" the child from her mother, she will alienate the mother. Communication between the parents is needed to encourage and support the mother with discipline while her daughter is in her care. This will foster harmony between all parents, discourage the child's manipulation and help her to feel secure in both homes.

Part Four

~~~~~~~~~

Secrets to
Successful Parenting

It's not possible to change your ancestry, but the decisions you make will impact your descendants!

The parent–child relationship is unique from any other. The biological and psychological ties form a tight bond. In healthy families, the parent-child experience is one of unconditional love. Children have a natural loyalty towards their biological parents whom they gain their sense of identity from. While stepparenting can be a difficult role, the practical advice and strategies included in this part can help you create harmonious relationships.

I get many stepparents telling me their spouse wants their current family to function in the same way a nuclear family does with both biological parents. Having gone through the death of a spouse or a broken relationship, they hope to recreate the experience of a nuclear family again by expecting the stepparent to fulfil all the roles and duties of a biological parent with the same passion. This is seldom possible. **We can expect a stepparent's relationship with a child to be different from a biological parent's, but not in a negative sense**. Children in blended families have the opportunity to benefit from and be positively influenced by all the adults in their life, be they blood related or not. They can grow to become well-adjusted healthy adults within the context of a blended family. **Blended families are unique in terms of dynamics but can operate as a supportive team.**

Strategy 1: Help for Biological Parents

Biological parents tend to look for and focus on the best attributes their children have to offer. It forms part of the unconditional love they have for their children. When others point out their child's shortcomings, a parent can feel threatened and jump to their child's defence. Stepparents will readily agree this is the case if they criticise a stepchild.

"Should I expect as much from my partner's children as I do from my own? Francine will go completely defensive if I say anything about her children. Is this normal? Francine's children are there 100% of the time and mine only 50%."

James

Age appropriate expectations should be the same for each child. Teachers will tell you some parents have great difficulty accepting that their child is anything less than perfect. Of course it is unrealistic to expect that any child is perfect. A parent who fails to recognise and assist their child through their weaknesses or mistakes will not equip them to reach their fullest potential in adulthood. Throughout life, others will not be as tolerant of their failures, so children must learn how to cope with them. It can also make life for the stepparent particularly difficult as they struggle with the pressure from the biological parent to accept behaviour that would in other situations not be tolerated.

Guilt
This topic was covered in depth in Part 3 (Strategy 2), so for now I will just reiterate a couple of points. If you have not had a look at Part 3, please do so.

Firstly, "There is no such thing as a perfect parent". At times we will fail our children, regardless of whether we are divorced or not. We must accept responsibility for those things we have control over, such as our contribution to a marriage breakdown or the failure to meet children's needs in other ways such as neglect, disciplining out of anger, or failing to support and encourage our children. Be assured that all of us experience failures however, we must forgive ourselves.

Secondly, we need to let go of the past and the guilt associated with it and plan for the future. **We can't change the past, but we can influence our future.**

Accept responsibility for your actions and their consequences, but focus on the future. Allowing guilt to motivate your parenting is destructive to the marriage relationship. Remember the sports field. How much respect would you have for a coach who never enforced rules, guideline or penalties just to keep some players happy? It certainly wouldn't build a successful and united team!

Feeling Torn

Why is it that biological parents go through the experience of feeling torn? Biological parents commonly recognise that their spouse will never love their child in the same manner as they do. With this realisation comes the responsibility to protect and defend their children from any outside influences they feel might threaten their children in some way.

Erin asks:
"What can I do to stop taking everything that happens to my daughter so personally? In other words, why do I feel the need to make an issue out of every little thing that happens to her? She seems to be fine with the way Nigel treats her...why does it bother me?"

A stepparent is never perceived as a threat so long as they are seen to be loving and devoted to a child. Unfortunately they can be on the back foot when it comes to confronting either the parent or child about a child's undesirable behaviour. Depending on how the stepparent tackles the situation, the biological parent's natural tendency will be to defend their children, in much the same way they would defend themselves when under attack. However, a parent may see him/herself as their child's only advocate. The stepparent may be seen as an adversary if they show anything other than love for a child. This can cause the parent to be very sensitive to criticism, particularly when they are unsure of the stepparent's motive.

If a parent believes a stepparent's behaviour is harmful or detrimental to their child, they will want to defend the child. This causes the stepparent to feel second. Consequently the parent feels pulled in two directions, trying to keep both the child and the stepparent happy.

"What if anything can I do to help this situation? I am at the point as to where I can not handle the stress anymore, I feel like I am being pulled in two different directions, and like I am being forced to make a decision between my child and my marriage."

Ben

It is very typical for children to cause strife in a couple's relationship. Ideally they want their biological parents to be together and a stepparent can be seen as an unwanted invasion. A child's feelings of anger and resentment can be displayed in disrespectful and defiant behaviour. Parents in blended families commonly form the perception that the children are destroying their relationship. They feel helpless in not being able to stop what becomes a destructive cycle of behaviour.

It is unfair to blame children entirely for the state of a couple's relationship. Yes, children create challenges for parents to work through, but they shouldn't be held responsible for how a couple chooses to deal with the challenges. In reality, the more significant issue is a couple's ability to find and agree on solutions for handling children's behaviour. Parents must endeavour to provide structure and security to help children come to terms with their blended family and discourage rebellious behaviour. If couples are proactive about improving their marriage, and accept the need to work together towards solutions, the children's behaviour will not destroy the relationship.

Our blended family will only be as strong as our marriage relationship; we need to focus on resolving conflict with our spouse by addressing the issues that cause the biological parent to feel torn. **If couples agree together on rules, expectations and roles, it will prevent opportunities arising that cause a biological parent to feel their loyalties are being divided.**

Loyalties
Sadly, in many blended families a parent will side in with their own child

over and above their spouse (see Part 3, Strategy 5). The following comments reflect some typical complaints:

"My husband compares our children and favours his."
"How do I avoid 'my child against yours'?"
"If my children do something wrong, my husband acts like it's my fault."

The conflicting loyalties bio parents experience in a blended family are inherent to the dynamics involved. **It is a reality of our family structure that at times we will feel the desire to defend our own offspring**. Some problems arise simply because of the dynamics. A problem cannot necessarily be blamed on one particular person. It may not be through any fault or provocation on behalf of our spouse that we feel the need to divide our loyalties; however, we must work honestly with them to process these feelings. We must accept that our family dynamics create an environment where loyalties will be tested.

Parents must address these issues if they want their family to function as a healthy team. We have talked about a bio parent's desire to defend and protect their child if they feel their child is threatened. It may not be behaviour problems that cause a division. A parent may feel threatened if their spouse's child is very successful in a particular area while their own child lags behind. Children will have strengths in different areas; to compare them in a negative sense is destructive for example, "My children would never do that!". If we think back to the sports field, the team will perform at its best when players are encouraged in their strengths and supported in their weaknesses. What kind of environment would be created if the player who scored the most runs or goals were to be alienated by a coach? Parent coaches must celebrate the successes of each child.

Success Strategy:
To create a supportive environment, **talk about the positive qualities in each other's children.** This will help diffuse unhealthy rivalry. You'll feel better about your children and each other.

If a child's problem behaviour divides a couple, a planned unified approach to discipline will be necessary to overcome the 'my child against yours' scenario. It can be very easy to let our emotions take over and control our response when we feel we are under attack. When tension is high over a problem concerning children, it is best to cool off before dealing with the issue. To maintain a child's respect for both parents, we must present a united front to them. Discuss these matters out of their hearing.

A note to stepparents: If you are struggling with an issue concerning the children, it's in your best interests to be sensitive in how you raise it; use the guidelines in Part 2.

Strategies for Bio Parents Who Feel Torn

- If a problem arises, avoid jumping to your children's defence; consider the facts along with the stepparent's viewpoint.
- Identify the problem; remember you're on the same team working towards the same goal.
- Stick to the facts and issue at hand; **leave emotion out of it.**
- Be fair; don't allow favouritism of your own child to dictate your response.
- Don't make excuses for your child's behaviour.
- Let the child take responsibility for their behaviour, not the parent.
- Work together towards resolving the problem so everyone feels satisfied with the outcome (Part 2).
- If you child was in the wrong, implement the consequences you and your spouse have agreed upon.
- If your child was the victim, encourage them to respond with grace to the offender.
- Ask your spouse what you want/need of them; remember they can't read your mind.

Your children will look to you for guidance on how they are to treat their stepparent. You must respect your spouse if you want your children to follow suit.

When problems arise between a stepparent and stepchild it can be tempting for the bio parent to resolve the matter and reconcile the relationship between the two. This may be appropriate from time to time initially (as long as they don't side with their child), but ultimately it's in a blended family's best interests for the stepparent and child to work through their differences together. It's the same with conflict between siblings; children must be taught peace making skills and have the opportunity to sort their differences out. If parents continually do it for them, children miss out on the valuable opportunity of learning how to resolve conflict for themselves. A parent can listen to each person without the need to jump in and fix the problem for them. Now back to stepparents and stepchildren; in the long run they too don't want to become dependent on the bio parent to sort their issues out.

As a biological parent, when do I feel torn between my spouse and children?

What will I do to avoid reacting defensively?

What can my spouse do to help me not feel torn?

Share your response with them.

Strategy 2: Positive Step Parenting

Parenting can be a rewarding and fulfilling experience in most cases. Step parenting can be the opposite when children resent the invasion of another adult in their lives. A blended family will function more effectively if family members' roles and expectations are clear to all. Step parenting is a joint venture. A stepparent is only in a child's life through their relationship with the bio parent. **A biological parent directly influences the stepparent's experience**. A stepparent depends on their spouse's support to succeed in their role. Ultimately, it is a bio parent's attitude and actions that dictate how effective a stepparent will be in his/her role. If a bio parent supports the stepparent, it will enhance the stepparent's experience almost regardless of the children's behaviour.

A stepmother or stepfather is the female or male head in the household. In an intact family, parents will easily perform tasks for their children that are taken for granted as their duty. The child is viewed as an extension of the parent who automatically does these tasks. In a blended family however, it cannot be assumed that a stepparent will serve their stepchildren in the same manner as a bio parents does often without recognition.

The most common complaints I hear from stepparents are:

- Feeling unappreciated for the practical role they perform
- Feeling powerless in decisions concerning their stepchildren
- Feeling their needs are second best to all others
- Feeling jealous or resentful of their stepchildren

The following comment from Nicky sums these up:

"I seem to have no say in my own house as to how I would like things done or help that I would like. The whole world revolves around my stepdaughter as she lives with us. My husband believes that I am asking him to choose when that's just not the case, I just want to have a bit of respect not only from his children but from him."

Nicky

If we feel like we have to serve others without a word of encouragement or appreciation in return, more often than not our attitude will turn to resentment.

You will be interested to know that the three top concerns in many blended families are:

- How to handle discipline
- Resolving conflict
- Dividing areas of responsibility

We have already covered the first two in some detail. It is the third point that I wish to emphasise in this part. If adults are clear about their role and children know what is expected of them, many potential problems will be avoided.

Adults must agree on their own roles and responsibilities as well as those for the children, and show appreciation.

People often don't mind helping practically, so long as their effort is appreciated. However, it's not uncommon for a spouse to act as though their partner's concerns are not important. They may not know how to respond to the situation, so it gets ignored in the hope that it will resolve itself. It could also be that a bio parent doesn't want to relinquish control or say over what happens to their children. Whatever the case, it is important for the stepparent to be brought on board as a team player so he/she can be recognised for their valuable contribution to family life. Think back to Part 2 on Conflict; issues that are left to build up cause walls of resentment and can blow up. These issues need to be addressed to have a healthy relationship.

Do I take my partner's parenting concerns seriously and work to resolve any issues?

What issues relating to my own or my partner's role/responsibilities do we need to resolve?

The following strategies are designed to help stepparents feel valued and supported in their role.

Strategies for Biological Parents:

- Verbally express how much you appreciate the valuable role and duties your partner performs as a stepparent.

- Keep your partner informed of what is happening in your children's lives, e.g. activities, interests, schooling, health, etc.

- Show you appreciate your partner by asking their opinion on matters concerning your children.

- Decide together the course of action.

- **Verbally affirm and support your partner in front of your children.**

- Encourage your children to express the same appreciation; it may just be to say "Thank you" for a meal prepared or a lift to an event.

- **Never** belittle or disrespect the stepparent in front of your children.

- Offer specific suggestions on how the stepparent can help your children feel accepted and important if this is an issue.

- Ask the stepparent what you can do to help them in their role.

- **Take seriously your partner's concerns; if it's important to them, it becomes important for the two of you to resolve.**

A bio parent's verbal support of the stepparent is essential if you want stepchildren to behave respectfully. The bio parent (being primarily responsible for enforcing consequences) needs to have a zero tolerance policy of disrespect from their children.

Can my children predict the consequences of being disrespectful?

What are the consequences of showing disrespect in our family?

A lot can be learned through our own parenting experience. For example, a person with a 10-year-old daughter might find they can readily connect with other girls up to that age but struggle to engage boys or teenage girls. While some people naturally have a gift for drawing children to them despite no parenting experience, others can find it a very difficult challenge. The following tips apply to all stepparents but may be particularly helpful for those who have not parented before.

Tips for stepparents who have never parented before

- Don't compete with the children; seek reassurance from your spouse if you are feeling second best.

- Agree on time spent alone without children and time spent with children.

- Seek direction from your spouse where you are unsure how to handle a behaviour or issue with a child.

- Watch and learn from your spouse about how to interact with the children at their age/stage.

- Give yourself and the child time to adjust to each other; bonding will happen over time.

- Be aware of your relationship as a stepparent and how your role differs from a biological parent.

- Problems can arise because of the step relationship. Don't take these personally or blame others; they may be inherent to blended family dynamics.

This last point is about recognising the unique role of the stepparent. Some problems can arise as a result of this relationship. It does not necessarily indicate a personality clash. Discipline is a good example; children can resent a stepparent disciplining them, for no reason other than they (the stepparent) do not have a biological connection. The stepparent should not take this as a personal insult or slight.

"The area that is not doing well is the relationship with my step-daughter. She has caused strife from the beginning and has tried to sabotage my relationship and marriage. She is rude, ignores me and is full of 'doom and gloom'. She says she doesn't like to be with us, but that is because she feels in competition with me for her father's attention. She is very against the idea of us having any more children."

Denise

Understanding the Difficult Stepchild

Both bio and stepparents need to appreciate that a child's behaviour can be a reflection of their feelings towards their family dynamics. A parent's remarriage can shatter any remaining hope they have for their biological parents' reconciliation. Unfortunately it is most often the stepparent who bears the brunt of a child's anger and resentment through defiant or disrespectful behaviour. Again, stepparents should not take this as an attack on them personally. The child's behaviour is a reflection of their feelings towards the situation. They could be defending their territory or fighting to regain the loss of their nuclear family.

I recall my feelings of resentment towards my own stepmother when my father remarried a year after my mother's death. She could have been any woman; it was not her personally that I resented, but the change and invasion of someone else. Over the following year we went on to develop a close friendship as she cared for and supported my brother and I. Although it was very hard for my stepmother to begin, the rough start did not prevent us from forming a great relationship!

We need to help children express their emotions or feelings in a positive manner. We've looked at those children who react adversely to their family environment, but there are also those whose behaviour seems too good to be true. A child's desire to see their parent happy and to be a part of a family again, may cause them to suppress their feelings or worries for fear of causing division. Children will feel anger, fear and uncertainty and must be encouraged to share these normal emotions. They have been through the turmoil of losing their biological parent's relationship and will need help and reassurance to cope with change.

Patience: A Crucial Secret to Success

"You can learn many things from children. How much patience you have, for instance."

Franklin P. Jones

Stepparents often identify patience as one thing they have learned from their experience. Patience requires self-control. It means not getting easily angered when something is out of line.

Using a couple of definitions for patience as a guide, this is the essence of what you need:

- A good-natured tolerance of delay or incompetence (www.wordnet. princeton.edu)
- The ability to endure waiting, delay, or provocation without becoming annoyed or upset, or to persevere calmly when faced with difficulties (www.wikipedia.org)
- A halo for sainthood if you can manage the above! ☺

It is necessary for stepparents to show patience and carefully considered responses towards their stepchildren to avoid conflict. If we react harshly towards our own children by raising our voice (yelling), we can naturally follow our failings up with a hug and apology. Our children will most likely accept this from us, in the same way we are ready to forgive them.

It's not quite as easy with stepchildren though. It can be much harder to mend the bridge when we are unsure how a stepchild will react, given they do not have the same endearment towards us as own children. It goes both ways: we may hold the hurt they cause us a little longer than we would with our own children. However, as the adult, stepparents must set the example and work to build on the relationship by showing patience. To show patience doesn't mean we ignore problems. **It's about planning our responses if we are unhappy with something and not allowing our emotions to dictate our actions.**

On a scale of **1** (Short tempered) to **5** (Very patient), how do you rate your level of patience?

Are you happy with your level?

Strategies to Increase Patience:

- Look after yourself; lack of food, sleep, and time out can cause irritability.

- Plan a time to reflect on or discuss an issue with your spouse before reacting.

- Tell yourself to relax; the world will not end.

- Build a strong marriage relationship; if your needs are being met within your relationship, you will experience less resentment towards your stepchildren and be more inclined to act patiently.

Responding with patience will help you build positive relationships with your stepchildren.

Conquering Resentment

It is not unusual for stepparents to feel uncomfortable or awkward around their stepchildren. This can come from not knowing how to respond or initiate interaction with them. One stepparent says:

"I do my best to not show I am uncomfortable with my stepchildren. I prefer they respect me rather than love me."

When we marry someone with children we are making a commitment to be a part of their children's lives, whether we like it or not. After all, children have a right to regular contact with both of their bio parents. However, despite an informed commitment, stepparents are still capable of feeling resentment towards children for the extra difficulties, work, and effort they require to meet these needs. Stepparents frequently find that life is much smoother and their marriage relationship happier when their stepchildren are not around. This is normal. The dynamics are not as complex and a couple can focus on each other. We all have a natural tendency to want to make life easier for ourselves by selfishly guarding against forces that threaten our relationship. Unfortunately, stepchildren can be perceived as such a force. When stepchildren are present, a couple's attention must be divided, there is an extra workload, and a couple may be required to have contact with the ex-partner through the child. Many couples will testify to the detrimental impact this alone can have on a relationship. See www. StepFamilyHelp.info for advice on this topic.

To feel resentment towards stepchildren can be natural. To have a healthy and successful blended family we must again, not blame children personally for this resentment. The resentment can be a direct result of the stepfamily dynamics. It's not necessarily a fault of your particular stepchildren. If you had different stepchildren you would most likely still have to deal with the same negative feelings.

If your spouse or stepchildren have particular behaviours that you struggle to deal with, you will need to address them to free yourself from resentment. Specifically identify the cause of your resentment. I remember one woman who strongly resented her stepdaughter, not because of anything the girl had done but because her husband treated his daughter like royalty and placed his wife's needs second. The issue is not about the daughter, but the husband. If a husband is willing to take time to make his wife feel loved and important it will enhance her feelings towards her stepchild. No longer will she need to feel threatened or resentful in her stepchild's presence. On a simpler note, it could be that a stepparent resents having to continually tidy up after his/her stepchildren. If this is the case, a stepparent needs to decide on a course of action in conjunction with their spouse so they do not have the responsibility of tidying up.

"How can I improve my relationship with my stepson? I harbour a lot of resentment and can't seem to forget and put it behind me. How do I get over the feeling that I don't want affection from him? I resent him and the time he takes away from my own son. How do I deal with that?"

Pam

It appears the resentment Pam feels is connected to the time and effort her stepson requires, which detracts from time she would rather spend with her own child. Her feelings may be well founded if she is left to be the primary caregiver for her stepson during visits. In reality, Pam must accept that her stepson will always require some of her time and attention. To help reduce her resentment, both she and her husband can look at ways of allowing her to have time alone with her own son. It would also be beneficial to negotiate ways of reducing her workload to a point where she felt comfortable with the demands of her role as a stepmother.

What causes you to feel resentment towards your stepchildren?

What can both you and your spouse do to help you overcome these feelings?

If we are clear about our role and the expectations within a family, there is less opportunity for conflict. Stepparents, particularly those new to the job, often struggle with how they fit in and what their role is. We recognise a stepparent does not replace a bio parent, so what is their role? Outlined below is a series of roles that a stepparent can fulfil to achieve a supportive and stable environment for the children in a blended family. These guidelines are broad enough to apply to all stepparents. You might like to take this opportunity to be more specific about your expectations. You can discuss for example, a stepparent's financial contribution or domestic duties.

The Role of a Stepparent:
- Accept and support stepchildren as part of your family.
- Be proactive in building the relationship with your stepchildren.
- Decide on house rules and consequences with the bio parent.
- Be honest if you are struggling; request your partner's help when you need it.

- Regularly communicate with your partner concerning their children's needs.
- Support your partner (the bio parent) to enforce consequences.
- Provide the male/female role model, head of the family.
- Support the child's relationship with their other biological parent (ex-partner).

As a stepparent, do you fulfil these roles in your home?

Are there areas you feel uncomfortable with?

Are there additional, more specific roles you would like to add?

Do you and your spouse agree on these roles?

What needs to happen for you to feel comfortable in these roles and how can your spouse help you?

Remember a great technique in conflict resolution is to **place yourself in your partner's position**. It always helps to see things from the other person's perspective. If you are a stepparent, ask yourself the following:

If your children had a stepparent, how would you want the stepparent to treat them?

Do I treat my stepchildren in the same way I would want my own children to be treated by a stepparent?

I occasionally get people asking me what name a stepparent should go by. Some children call their stepparent mum or dad, which is fine if the stepchild initiates this. It is more common where the other bio parent is absent from the child's life. Where regular contact is maintained with both biological parents, it may not be appropriate unless the child feels strongly about it.

The main point I want to emphasise here is to **act with the child's best interests** at heart. Some stepparents want to be called mum or dad because it makes them feel good. However, if this causes the child to feel disloyal or creates friction with the other biological parent, it should be avoided. Give the child the option; ask them how they wish to refer to the stepparent.

If you feel after reading this section that either party may be uncomfortable with the current name/term, you may wish to address the subject with your stepchildren. Work out a term each person feels at ease with.

Some Encouragement
I love the following comment from Paul. It shows how children do not necessarily have an appreciation of the difficult role their stepparent takes on until they themselves go through a similar scenario as an adult.

"It's so hard to love and treat other children like your own. I have a stepfather myself and now know how difficult it must have been on him. I admire him so much for sticking to it for the past 30 years. His example keeps me going even though I feel like giving up."

Paul

Speaking from my own experience as a stepchild, I can now look back and identify the difficulties my own stepmother faced. Now that I appreciate her difficulties, I can understand the motive behind her actions, and how hard it must have been at times. Yes, the role of a stepparent can be a difficult and thankless one, often without the immediate rewards that a bio parent experiences. Be assured that despite the difficulties you may currently face, you can in time form an amicable and even a loving relationship with your stepchildren through using the strategies shared in this part.

"Always bear in mind that your own resolution to succeed is more important than any other one thing."

Abraham Lincoln

Strategy 3: Meeting Children's Needs

Time is perhaps the most precious commodity we have to dispose of. Each moment that passes can never be repeated. Use it wisely and you will reap the benefits at a future time; waste it away, and you will see little gain in your life. We have talked about the importance of making time for our spouse if we are to enjoy a healthy relationship. We'll now look at the issue of time with our children.

Quality time with a person is necessary if we desire to build a significant relationship. You may have heard the saying "It's quality, not quantity that counts". Unfortunately, this isn't exactly true. If relationships are to remain strong and intimate, a balance of both quality and quantity is needed. You might be thinking, "But I don't see .... for years and when we catch up it's like nothing has changed". This is probably because your relationship with this person was deepened by many shared experiences and time spent together initially. In many cases however, going lengths of time without seeing a friend causes the relationship to drift apart.

In families where an ex-partner has sole custody, it may not be possible to spend much 'quantity' time with children. If this is the case for you, regular contact through phone, email or letters to your children shows them you care and encourages the ongoing growth of the relationship. When children come to visit they will need to spend time together with their family, including stepparents and siblings, plus individual time with their bio parent.

In our family, we try to spend some focused time alone with each child to connect with them on a more intimate level about what is happening in their life. It is seldom possible to make this kind of connection in a group setting. In a blended family, **children still need quality individual time with their bio parent to strengthen and affirm this primary relationship**. Stepparents need to encourage their partner to find these opportunities. Some stepparents naturally struggle with this because the relationship between the parent and child can make them feel like an unwelcome outsider. These feelings may be justifiable if a parent's attention is solely devoted to their child through the duration of the visit, neglecting all else. Try to include visiting children in the normal household routines so they feel part of the family, not just an outsider. A realistic balance including time with our spouse will help build a family team.

"My spouse will not include us when he has time with his daughter – we always include him. I am jealous that my husband spends time with his daughter but doesn't want to spend any with my family."

Camilla

Camilla feels her husband is being unfair. However, it's ok for both her and her husband to have time alone with their respective children. Camilla's husband's unwillingness to spend time with her family is a separate matter. Camilla must communicate with her husband how she feels about his apparent lack of interest. They will need to discuss and plan for some fun activities they can all enjoy together as a family.

"My stepchild is very insecure and needy. He wines, clings and manipulates his Mom and Dad. Once he is here he pouts and mopes and follows his Dad around like a shadow."

This child feels most secure in his father's company but may be unsure about where he fits in relation to the other family members. His father can help him identify and discuss his feelings about his new environment. Including this child in family activities will help him become familiar with his role and the expectations the parents (bio and step) set. If he's given the opportunity to choose a family activity, and praised for his contribution, it will set the scene for him to feel more involved in family life.

It's clear that many stepparents struggle to form a relationship with their stepchildren. In some cases the stepparent may prefer not to have a relationship with a stepchild.

"Is it normal to find this situation so difficult? I feel so very resentful and guilty for the resentment I feel. I am happy for my partner to spend as much time with his son as he wants, does that mean I have to too? I feel like such a horrible person."

Jackie

During visitation, stepparents should not feel as though they need to stick around all the time. They can take the opportunity to enjoy some time for themselves and allow the bio parent to have some focused time with their children. However, stepparents will still need to spend some time with their stepchild (not necessarily alone) to foster the relationship building process.

Equal Treatment

Stepparents often share a common and natural tendency to treat their stepchildren differently from their biological children. They can either be much harsher on them, or too soft, being scared to ask for or encourage compliance with rules. In the first case, it can be easier to have higher expectations of someone else's child than your own because you do not have the same compassion or unconditional love towards the child that a bio parent enjoys. In the latter case it can be easier to avoid a potential problem by not seeking compliance to begin with. For example, it might be much easier to do a chore yourself as a stepparent than risk asking a stepchild to do it and have them refuse. With a bio child you automatically inherit the right to discipline as part of the expectation that it is in the child's best interests. However, there is no such right/expectation for stepparents. The following comment from one stepmother's experience is an honest reflection of the feelings many stepparents go through.

"I love my own children more than anything. The love you have for your own biological children could never compare with that for your steps. I would run out in front of a bus for them..... Some days I could push my stepchildren out in front of a bus! Just jokes but there lay the difference."

Parents share a natural tendency to put the needs or interests of their own children before those of their spouse's children. While we must endeavour to treat all children equally within a family, most parents experience the inherent urge to favour their own children. This is a typical reflection of the dynamics at work within a blended family.

"My partner treats his child differently from mine; their needs come before ours."

The most common complaint I hear is that a spouse is more lenient on his/her own children compared to their stepchildren. The following case illustrates how this can cause havoc in a relationship.

"Ben disciplines my son Ethan but not his own. He tries to discipline Ethan harshly but then allows his own son to do exactly the same thing. If I go and get some clothes for Ethan, Ben has to make sure he gets same or better to show us. When I shop I mainly get for both kids, but he will only shop for his son. Ben's son tells his father I'm mean if I make him pick up toys so then he gets down on Ethan more, and tells me I am mean and hard on his son."

We have covered the topic of discipline and reasons for having the same clear age appropriate rules and expectations for each child. Some blended families benefit from formalising a united approach towards the areas of discipline, time, activities and money spent on children. This goal of this approach to is ensure children within the family are treated equally. So how does it work?

The Consensus Contract: A secret to success

The concept of a Consensus Contract is simple; a couple agree together how the following areas will work. This ensures they make each other's interests their first concern. After discussion, a spouse can only act in the areas they have agreed upon.

Discipline: What is each parent's role in enforcing the age appropriate boundaries and expectations for every child (identified in Part 3)?

Time: How much time should each parent (biological and step) aim to spend with a child every week?

Money: How should money be spent on meeting each child's needs? Should each have a planed allowance for clothing, presents, sports, music, tuition, holiday programs, and entertainment? Should it be based on current needs?

Activities: Should outings include all children? Is it acceptable for one child to have an outing with a parent and not include the others? How many extra-curricular activities should a child get involved in? What if one has many interests and another child doesn't have any?

"How do I get Chris to understand that things are not going to be totally equal between his kids and mine; his kids don't live here. I want to do fun things with my kids. He thinks we should wait until they are all together. But, his kids do things with their mom, so why shouldn't mine get the same?"

Jenny

Both Chris and Jenny are right to some extent. Jenny's life with her children should not be put on hold while Chris's children are with their mother. However, it is still important when everyone is together to enjoy activities that will build cohesiveness and positive memories.

Now it's your chance to think about how to approach these areas. **The goal of the Consensus Contract is to reach wholehearted agreement on a course of action before proceeding.** You may or may not feel the need to write a formal plan for each area, depending on whether the questions reflect a source of conflict within your relationship. It may be enough that you make a commitment to prioritise each other's interests by discussing issues together and working towards solutions.

Do you and your spouse feel your family would benefit from a Consensus Contract?

Together write and sign a Consensus Contract below stating you will work together to reach wholehearted agreement before acting on matters concerning the children in your family.

As you work through the following questions you might like to utilize the skills and principles outlined in Part 2:

- Use reflective listening.
- Identify each other's feelings and perspective.
- Be creative in identifying possible solutions.
- Make each other's interests paramount when deciding on a solution.

Have you both agreed on each parent's role in discipline (Part 3)?

Write your decision here.

How do you both feel about spending individual time with biological children? Is this something you want to plan for?

Look at the area of money and decide on the basis of spending for each child.

Decide how activities should be approached in your family.

Strategy 4: How to Bond with Stepchildren

When we marry someone with children, we make the decision to become a significant part of their children's lives. This is our choice. Children however, do not have such a choice and for many reasons may resent the invasion, making it hard for a stepparent to form a bond. They have already experienced loss in their lives and may be fearful of losing a parent to a stepparent. A child might push a stepparent away to protect their relationship with their bio parent. Stepparents may resent their stepchild's grief and insecurity, driving them further apart. The relationship between a child and their stepparent will develop by choice. In this strategy we will look at how to build this key relationship.

A Child's Loyalty

Children will feel secure within their relationships if they have both biological parents' permission to love the other, and to like the stepparent. If the ex-partner runs the stepparent down, all is not lost providing the bio parent affirms their spouse (stepparent). Children feel caught in the middle if parents run each other down in front of them. Avoid doing this yourself at all costs as it is harmful to a child's psychological well-being and sense of security. If you know an ex-partner is guilty of this, reassure your child that both parents love them and want the best for them. Be aware that it is common for children to feel they are being disloyal to the absent bio parent (ex-partner) if they form a positive relationship with a stepparent. Give children permission to like their stepparent. Let children know they are not being disloyal to the absent parent, as the stepparent is not trying to replace them.

You can't control what happens in the ex-partner's home, but you can control what happens in your home. Explain to your child that in your home each person must treat others with respect. Make it a policy in your home that you do not speak negatively about the ex-partner in front of a child. If a stepparent shows an unfavourable attitude towards the ex-partner, it can cause a child to withdraw for fear of being disloyal to their other bio parent.

"How can I love my stepson and not divide his loyalty to his mom or make my children feel slighted?"

Tammy

When a stepparent supports a child's relationship with the ex-partner (other parent), a child is less likely to feel they're being disloyal to them by forming a bond with their stepparent. Help children avoid feeling like they have to side with either parent. Step and bio parents can do this by:

- Affirming the ex-partner; tell your child they have a great mother/father who also wants the best for them.

- Normalising the child's feelings; tell your child it is normal for them to feel they are being disloyal to their other parent by having a relationship with the stepparent.

- Assure your child that it's ok to have a good relationship/friendship with the stepparent who does not want to take the place of the other parent.

A Parent's Loyalty

A parent may also feel they are being disloyal to their own children if they form a strong connection with their stepchildren. A parent can fear his or her own child will feel neglected or less important. It can prevent them as a stepparent from actively encouraging the bonding process with a child. There are two things to note if this applies in your household. Firstly, it must be clear to all that both bio and step children share the same rights, rules, and privileges. If children see they are treated in a fair and consistent manner, they will feel more secure with the dynamics. Secondly, all children in a home have the right to feel welcome and cared for by the adults, but the emotional tie will almost always be stronger between a bio parent and child. Parents should not feel guilty about this natural dynamic, but neither should they feel guilty about forming a relationship with a stepchild.

Relationships Need Time

As we discovered already, it can take seven or more years to fully integrate as a family unit or genuinely united team. Be patient when building a relationship with your stepchild. If you expect a deep loving relationship to happen quickly, chances are you will be disappointed. Try not to pressure stepchildren into a relationship with you. Allow them to set the pace. If they respond to you with affection, show a willingness to give and receive it. Don't force the relationship but respect their feelings. The time it takes for these relationships to develop may be particularly hard for bio parents when they want those they love the most to love each other. However, bio parents must accept that time is needed and avoid laying blame when things do not happen as quickly as they would like. The length of time needed to form a bond is a result of the step dynamics. It does not necessarily reflect any personal inadequacy.

"I do not seem to get myself closer to her (stepdaughter) to get to know her. I'm very reserved and do not speak to her often. I do not want to baby sit her or be alone with her with out her father."

Elizabeth

For a relationship to grow, two people must spend time together and show an interest in the other's lives. A stepparent may be hesitant to reach out to a child for fear of rejection. Some are uncomfortable with children or unsure about how to behave around them. Children are egocentric and therefore will not necessarily be proactive in showing any interest in another person's life. Bio parents must therefore take responsibility for instigating and role modelling the behaviour they hope to encourage in their children. In such cases the bio parent's understanding, support and encouragement is necessary because again, it will take time for the stepparent to feel comfortable and form a bond with a child.

Steps for Stepparents
- Affirm the ex-partner.
- Approach the relationship with your partner's children as a friend.
- Appreciate your role will evolve; avoid disciplining especially in the initially stages of the relationship, have more of a babysitter role where you are given authority from the bio parent.
- You will have to work towards having a respectful relationship before a loving relationship develops.

- Enjoy group activities to begin; it can be less threatening for the two of you than time alone.

- If you **both** feel comfortable having time alone, seek opportunities to interact and enjoy an activity (e.g. watch a movie, play a game) together.

- Keep informed about what is going on in their life such as interests, school commitments, friendships, etc., so you have a basis for conversation.

- Look at the child as an individual rather than 'your spouse's child'.

- Be patient, you may need to give a child time to adjust to having you as a part their life before they will allow you into their life.

- Empathise with their experience of loss.

- Avoid coming on strong; **let the child set the pace.**

- Show openness for affection but don't thrust yourself into their space.

- Be sensitive to their response to you; don't probe them about personal issues or details unless they appear willing to have an intimate conversation.

- Take the initiative in conversation; ask about your stepchild's day and take an interest in their activities.

- Share your own interests or experiences with your stepchildren.

- Don't be too hard on yourself; a bond takes time so failure to form one quickly despite trying, does not reflect any inadequacy on your behalf.

- Encourage and compliment your stepchildren, it will go a long way in fostering positive feelings towards you.

Conversation Starters
- "I'd love to hear what you've been doing today."
- "Tell me about …. (an interest)."
- "I hear you've achieved … that's awesome, how did it feel?"

- "Your father/mother and I are planning a family outing, what are your thoughts on where we should go?"

- "When I was a child I enjoyed watching ... Have you heard of it? What is your favourite program to watch?"

- "I'd enjoy hearing what you're learning about in science at the moment."

- "Who's your favourite teacher, friend ....?"

- "Have you heard about ... (news worthy item)? What are people at school saying about it?"

While I've shared many bonding strategies for a stepparent to use, bio parents must play and active part in this process too. This is particularly important if a stepparent becomes the target of a child's anger as Colin shares:

"My child blames his stepmother for my divorce and has a deep anger towards her."

Colin

Reassure your child it is normal to feel angry their parents are no longer together, but it's not one person's fault. Avoid laying blame. Below are some strategies that bio parents can use to encourage their child's relationship with a stepparent:

Strategies for Biological Parents

- Speak positively about the stepparent.

- Talk to your child about their feelings towards the stepparent; **they are someone else to love them, not make their life more difficult.**

- Let your child know it's natural for them to feel loyal towards their bio parent, but it's still ok for them to have a positive relationship with the stepparent.

- Spend some time alone with them so they don't feel the need to compete for your attention.

- A child may not feel any love for a stepparent but must show respect; encourage them to respond positively to a stepparent's warmth, i.e. answer questions without icy stares or silence.

The strategies outlined will not necessarily come easily or automatically

Like any relationship, we have to work at them. Below are two examples where a stepparent struggles with liking their stepchildren. The first is from Nancy's perspective as a stepparent; the second is from Tracey's perspective as a bio parent.

"I try my hardest to not let my stepchildren know I have bad feelings for them. I am pretty sure they sense my frustration though. I have worked with other people's children for a long time and I never thought I could feel so badly towards another child. Being a stepparent is hard on the heart."

Nancy

"Right now Megan is very unhappy. She wants to live with her dad, but she knows he really doesn't want her. She wishes Rick (step dad) could show her more love and affection, like he does his own daughter. I truly love him and he is the best thing that has happened to me, besides having my children. I just wish he and Megan could get along. Sometimes it seems he doesn't like her. He is always on her "case". She knows it and feels it. She feels unloved and rejected by her bio dad and Rick her step dad."

Tracey

In most cases it is unrealistic to expect a stepparent to love a child in the same way they would love a bio child. A realistic expectation is that respect and friendship will grow between a child and stepparent over time. In my experience, most stepparents don't feel the amount of love they think they should towards stepchildren. Firstly, this is very normal so don't beat yourself up about it. The absence of the 'feeling of love' does not make someone a bad stepparent; in fact they can still be a fantastic stepparent! Secondly, love can be an action; it doesn't have to be a feeling. You can rise above your feelings by behaving kindly towards stepchildren as you are presented with opportunities.

Think of a teacher in a class room; seldom can they say they 'like' every child they teach. What they can do is look for the best in each child (yes, even the most challenging ones) and encourage them. So, they can be a great teacher even though they may not warm to every child. If you're a stepparent, try to be sincere and encourage children in their strengths. It can take years for stepparents to 'feel' love, so there's no need to feel bad or guilty; give yourself plenty of time. Choose your attitude. Don't wait to have positive feelings before you act in a kind manner. As adults it is our responsibility to take the initiative to build the relationship.

We've now covered many reasons stepparents resent the 'invasion' of stepchildren. Most often it is because they feel they have to compete for their spouse's attention. Remember as a couple to consider each other's needs and spend quality time together. If you're a stepparent, respect that children are entitled to the time effort and energy a bio parent gives to meet their needs. Focus on building a solid relationship (Part 1) and you'll enjoy the benefits of being able to smooth out the parenting issues.

Finally, we must tell our spouse specifically how they can help us in our role as a parent/stepparent and what they can do to help our children (if relevant) feel accepted and important. Ask them what they need from us in return.

Here are some final words of encouragement from two stepparents.

"In the beginning, I had MUCH conflict with my stepson Phillip. He is strong willed and ALL boy. I really just didn't like him. I cried and cried and prayed and prayed. Our relationship is much better now he has matured and grown. It's still not perfect, but much, much better!! I actually love him. He is a great kid!"

"I feel you have to first earn the trust and respect of your new stepchildren, and build a relationship from there. Everyone wants the new home to be comfortable, and for the children to realise that the stepparent is one more person to love them, and not to make their lives more difficult."

We've covered four fundamental parts to achieving long-term success in a blended family environment. Remember relationships take time and patience to develop. Don't expect your family to operate in the same way as a nuclear family (both bio parents). We know that as a family we'll continue to face challenges but if we uphold grace and forgiveness as core values, we can work through the challenges and come out stronger from them. Celebrate the opportunity for all family members to learn and benefit from each other in a supportive team environment. You can enjoy blended family success!

Closing Comment

You will most likely have picked up many skills and strategies throughout this book that have benefited my family and hundreds of others world wide. Here's your opportunity to read about one other element in my life that has helped me through the tough times and been responsible for much of the wisdom I have shared with you. If you want to know more, read on.

On a human level we can do and say all the right things to have a successful family life but I believe it's God who has been at work in my family to ultimately bring strength and hope to us through the hard times. I've had times where I've struggled to be patient (yes, I've even 'lost it' on the odd occasion), but I've always known that ultimately God is there ready to help me. I've had to ask Him for this help and the vision to write this book came to me one day when I was praying for assistance.

You see, I don't claim to be perfect or know everything. My faith hasn't protected me from challenges, but one thing is for sure, it's got me through them. When I'm faced with the choices I've made (both the good and bad) I know that God is always with me through the consequences. God promises never leave or forsake us but will lovingly guide us in His ways if allow him.

I believe God loves me and everyone he created. The Bible says that God can bring good into our lives out of situations that might otherwise leave us 'worse for wear'. All we need to do is ask God for help and place our trust in Him. God loves us unconditionally with a father's heart and nothing can ever separate us from this love.

"For God so loved the world that he gave his only Son, so that everyone who believes in him will not perish but have eternal life. God did not send his Son into the world to condemn it, but to save it."

John 3 v 16-17

For more information go to:
www.family.org/faith/A000000883.cfm

Alternatively you can visit my website **www.StepFamilyHelp.info** and contact me via email.

Bibliography

Adkins, K. *I'm Not Your Kid: A Christian's Guide to a Healthy Stepfamily.* Grand Rapids: Baker Books, 2004.

Burns, Cherie. *Stepmotherhood.* New York: Three Rivers Press, 2001.

Deal, Ron L. *The Smart Step Family.* Minnesota: Bethany House, 1996.

Doerken, Maurine. *Stepparenting Without Guilt.* Nevada City: Blue Dolphin Publishing, Inc., 2000.

H. Norman Wright. *Before You Remarry.* Oregon: Harvest House Publishers, 1999.

Lofas, Jeannette. *Stepparenting.* New York: MJF Books, 1995.

Sturt, John and Agnes. *Mentoring for Marriage.* Auckland: DayStar Publications Trust, 2004.

Wagner/Gruen. *Strategies for a Successful Marriage.* Colorado Springs: Nav Press, 1994.

About the Author

Adele Cornish is the mother of three boys and has been the stepmother of two children for fourteen years. She's also a step daughter (her father remarried after her mother's death). After experiencing challenges in her own blended family, Adele developed a vision for helping others in a similar position. She has spent years utilising her social work background to extensively research and address the unique challenges blended families face.

Adele has used this knowledge and her experience to develop a program that currently teaches practical skills and strategies to hundreds of couples worldwide, equipping them to overcome the common obstacles to blended family success (see Testimonials on inside cover). She has appeared on national television (the Good Morning Show) here in New Zealand speaking on the topic of blended families.

Visit her website **www.StepFamilyHelp.info** to receive free weekly tips and information on the following topics:

- How to Help Your Children Thrive in a Blended Family

- Ex Partners & In-laws: Building the bridge of peace

- Personality Profiling: Discover your personality type

- Help to Heal After Divorce

For ongoing in-depth support and advice, go to:

www.StepFamilyHelp.info

Notes

Notes